KU-470-029

At the age of nineteen, **Kenny McGovern** was diagnosed with what's known as 'Social Anxiety Disorder' and eventually became too ill to carry on working. As the years passed, he became almost housebound as a result of his illness and as such lost touch with many parts of life, which although enjoyable are often taken for granted. Simple pleasures such as buying a nice sandwich from a local café or going out for a meal became impossible for him to do.

As a result of this, and because of his love of food and cooking, he eventually took to trying to recreate many of his favourite shop-bought foods at his Glasgow home. 'If I can't go to McDonald's, I'll make my own,' was his philosophy. Over a period of five years or more, he tested and tweaked many, many recipes, his new hobby quickly building into an obsession.

In 2010 Kenny decided to publish some selected recipes in his first book, *The Takeaway Secret* – it became an instant bestseller, following word-of-mouth recommendations on the Internet. In this new edition he has refined many of the original recipes and introduced many new ones.

Other titles

The Street Food Secret
The Busy Mum's Plan-ahead Cookbook
Eat Well, Spend Less
The Healthy Lifestyle Diet Cookbook
The Everyday Halogen Oven Cookbook
Slow Cook, Fast Food
The Air Fryer Cookbook
Superfood Soups

The Takeaway Secret

Kenny McGovern

....

2nd Edition

ROBINSON

First published in Great Britain
in 2017 by Robinson

10 9 8 7 6 5 4 3 2

Copyright © Kenny McGovern, 2017

The moral right of the author
has been asserted.

All rights reserved.
No part of this publication may be
reproduced, stored in a retrieval system,
or transmitted, in any form, or by any
means, without the prior permission
in writing of the publisher, nor be
otherwise circulated in any form of
binding or cover other than that in which
it is published and without a similar
condition including this condition being
imposed on the subsequent purchaser.

A CIP catalogue record for this book
is available from the British Library.

ISBN: 978-1-47214-005-0

Typeset in New Caledonia by
Hewer Text UK Ltd, Edinburgh

Printed and bound in Great Britain by
CPI Group (UK) Ltd, Croydon CR0 4YY

Papers used by Robinson are
from well-managed forests and
other responsible sources.

Robinson
An imprint of
Little, Brown Book Group
Carmelite House
50 Victoria Embankment
London EC4Y 0DZ

An Hachette UK Company
www.hachette.co.uk

www.littlebrown.co.uk

Notes on the recipes:
The recipes give metric and imperial
measurements – use one or other
system, but not a mixture of both. Always
use medium-size eggs and vegetables,
unless stated otherwise. Herbs are
fresh, unless stated otherwise.

Contents

Introduction

When *The Takeaway Secret* was published in 2010, it was the culmination of years of investigation into secret recipes and ingredients used by fast-food and takeaway chefs. I was delighted that my recipes had been published and was overwhelmed by the reaction of readers who enjoyed them. The support and encouragement I've received, both in relation to my recipes and to my experiences with Social Anxiety Disorder, has been so positive, and I'll always be grateful that so many people took the time to get in touch. If you'd like to discuss Social Anxiety Disorder, or just send me a picture of the pizza you made that night, I'll always be glad to hear from you.

Some years on from the original publication of *The Takeaway Secret*, I hope that I can now offer even more insights into some of the secret recipes and cooking techniques used, as well as some new dishes such as King Prawn with Ginger & Spring Onion, or the famous Scottish Pizza Crunch. Should you try the recipes included in this revised book, I hope you'll be glad to have done so.

PART 1

American Fast Food

The USA is arguably the king of fast food. Certainly, the Americans are responsible for the slick, quick turnaround system that we see in every major town and city throughout the world today. That consistent product brought to you with speedy service is the fast-food model now mimicked across the entire food industry.

And fast food isn't just about snacking. Large chains offer menus based entirely around breakfast, lunch or dinner, as well as everything in between. Despite the ever-growing number of fast-food chains, however, the US also benefits from thousands of well-established 'mom-n-pop' or family owned restaurants and cafés.

Food is big business and the rivalry between the biggest brands is fierce. This can be excellent news for consumers, as the range of special menu items and new products offers more for the fast-food fan to experience. Of course, many people have their own favourite chains and so if your favourite restaurant does things a certain way, you'll be able to apply those techniques when you make your own dishes at home.

Thanks to the diverse cultures and peoples who make up the USA, fast food is reflective of a wide range of food history and so variety is the spice of life. From breakfast pancakes and muffins to burgers and fried chicken, making up your mind from a menu of American fast food can prove tricky indeed!

Egg Muffin (American Fast-food Style)

SERVES 1
1 English muffin, halved
1 teaspoon butter, plus extra for greasing
1 slice of processed cheese
1 egg

1 Preheat the oven to its lowest setting.
2 Heat a dry frying pan over a medium heat. Toast the muffin halves cut-side down in the pan for around 30 seconds or until golden. Remove the pan from the heat.
3 Spread the toasted muffin halves with butter while they are still warm and place the processed cheese slice on the bottom half, then set aside.
4 Add a little oil to the pan and put it back on the heat. Using a greased egg ring, crack an egg into the pan and immediately burst the yoke with a knife. Cover the egg ring with a square of foil and cook on a low–medium heat for 2–3 minutes or until the yolk is just beginning to set.
5 Remove the foil and the egg ring and flip the egg. Cook on the other side for a further 1 minute.
6 Remove the pan from the heat, slide the egg onto the cheese-topped muffin half and top with the muffin lid.
7 Wrap the filled muffin in greaseproof paper or foil, then place it in the oven and warm through for 3–4 minutes. Serve immediately.

Variations

BACON AND EGG MUFFIN
Add two slices of cooked Canadian bacon inside the muffin.

SAUSAGE AND EGG MUFFIN
Add one American Breakfast Sausage (see p.4).

American Breakfast Sausage (American Fast-food Style)

SERVES 1

About 55g/2oz pork mince

½ teaspoon dried sage

¼ teaspoon brown sugar

A little vegetable oil, for frying

Sea salt and freshly ground black pepper

1   Put the pork, sage and sugar in a bowl, season with a pinch each of salt and pepper, and use your hands to combine thoroughly.

2   Roll the pork mixture into a ball, place it on a sheet of greaseproof paper, then place another sheet over the top. Flatten the ball between the two sheets into a thin circular patty, slightly bigger than the size of an English muffin. Place the patty, covered, in the coldest part of the fridge for 1–2 hours, or leave it overnight so that it's ready to cook in the morning.

3   When you're ready to cook, heat a splash of vegetable oil in a frying pan over a low–medium heat. Place the sausage patty into the pan and cook for about 3 minutes per side, or until cooked through and golden all over.

4   Remove the sausage patty from the pan and drain off any excess oil on kitchen paper. Serve with pancakes and scrambled eggs as part of a big breakfast, or added to an Egg Muffin (see p.3).

Bacon, Cheese & Folded Egg Omelette Bagel (American Fast-food Style)

In recent years US fast-food restaurants have expanded breakfast menus considerably. A breakfast bagel is the perfect start to the day – here's how to faithfully recreate the fast-food classic.

SERVES 1

1 bagel, halved
2 teaspoons margarine
2 slices of processed cheese
2 slices of lean unsmoked back bacon
1 egg
2 tablespoons semi-skimmed milk
½ teaspoon vegetable oil
Sea salt and freshly ground black pepper

1 Preheat the grill to medium–high and the oven to its lowest setting.
2 Place the bagel slices cut-side up on the grill pan and toast under the grill for about 2 minutes, until golden.
3 Place the bagel halves on a sheet of foil and spread each half with 1 teaspoon of margarine, then top with a slice of processed cheese.
4 Grill the bacon for about 5–6 minutes, until cooked through, turning once during cooking. Place both bacon slices on top of one bagel half.
5 In a small bowl, whisk together the egg and semi-skimmed milk to combine thoroughly.
6 Heat a non-stick wok or frying pan over a high heat. Add the vegetable oil. Pour half of the egg–milk mixture into the pan, then season with a pinch each of sea salt and pepper. Tilt the pan if

necessary in order to let any uncooked mixture move around the pan and cook.

7   Carefully slide a thin spatula underneath the cooked egg mixture and shake the pan forcefully until the egg omelette moves freely around the pan. Use the spatula to flip the omelette or, if you're feeling brave, toss the omelette in the pan. Cook the other side for 20–30 seconds and remove onto a plate. Repeat the process with the remaining egg mixture, if you wish.

8   Fold the egg omelette in half and then in half again and place it on top of the bacon, then top with the bagel-and-cheese lid.

9   Wrap the bagel loosely in foil or baking paper and place it in the oven at the lowest available setting for 3–4 minutes to heat through and allow the flavours to mingle. Serve with Mini Hash Browns (see p.8).

Breakfast Pancakes (American Fast-food Style)

MAKES 8 PANCAKES
120g/4oz self-raising flour
Pinch of sea salt
30g/1oz caster sugar
1 egg
140ml/¼ pint whole milk, plus extra if necessary
Vegetable oil, for greasing

1   In a large bowl, combine the flour and sea salt. Add the sugar and mix well.
2   In a separate bowl, combine the egg and milk, then pour the wet into the dry ingredients and whisk thoroughly to create a smooth, slightly thick batter. Add a little more milk if necessary.
3   Lightly grease a frying pan with vegetable oil and place over a medium–high heat. Drop one ladleful of the pancake batter into the pan at a time. Allow the pancake to cook for 50–60 seconds or until bubbles cover the pancake, then use a flat spatula to flip the pancake over and continue to cook on the other side for a further 30–40 seconds, until both sides are golden brown.
4   Remove from the pan and set aside. Repeat the cooking process until you have used up all the batter. Serve as part of a big breakfast with scrambled eggs and American Breakfast Sausage (see p.4), or with cooked bacon and maple syrup.

Mini Hash Browns

These crispy potato bites are the perfect breakfast side dish.
American fast-food chains use specially designed machine
moulds in order to create their hash browns. This recipe
recreates that machinery using simple ice-cube trays!

SERVES 2–3 (MAKES ABOUT 42)

4 large potatoes
1 teaspoon sea salt, plus an extra pinch
1 teaspoon butter
Large pinch of black pepper
¼ teaspoon white sugar
1 egg
6 tablespoons plain flour
Vegetable oil, for deep frying

1   Peel the potatoes and place them whole in a large pan of water. Add
    a pinch of sea salt and bring to the boil over a high heat. Allow the
    potatoes to boil for around 5–6 minutes, then drain and set aside.
2   When the potatoes have cooled to room temperature, place them in
    a food-safe bag and refrigerate for 1 hour until cold.
3   Remove the potatoes from the fridge, then grate into a large bowl.
    Add the sea salt, butter, black pepper, sugar, egg and flour and use
    your hands to mix thoroughly until fully combined. The mixture
    should become very sticky.
4   Fill the moulds of ice-cube trays with the mixture until you have
    used it all up (you'll need about 42 little moulds altogether), then
    place the trays in the freezer and leave overnight to freeze.
5   When you're ready to cook the hash browns, set your deep fryer
    to 180°C/350°F. Alternatively, fill a wok or large frying pan one
    third full with vegetable oil and heat to 180°C/350°F. The oil is
    ready when a few breadcrumbs dropped into the oil sizzle
    immediately.

6 Push out the frozen mini hash browns from the ice-cube trays and into a large bowl. Use a large metal spoon to drop a few hash browns at a time into the hot oil, to fry in batches for about 3 minutes per batch. Remove the hash browns from the oil using a slotted spoon and set aside on a plate for 2 minutes. This will allow the potato to continue cooking on the inside without too much browning.

7 Return the mini hash browns to the oil and fry for a further 2–3 minutes or until golden, crispy and cooked through. Remove from the pan, drain off any excess oil and repeat until you have cooked all the hash browns. Serve with Bacon, Cheese & Folded Egg Omelette Bagels (see p.5).

Meatball Sub (American Fast-food Style)

This recipe makes enough meatballs and marinara sauce for three sandwiches. The meatballs and sauce freeze well for up to 3 months – so, enjoy them with your friends straightaway, or freeze in portions for another time.

MAKES 3 SANDWICHES
2 slices of white bread, crusts removed
½ teaspoon dried Italian herbs
2 garlic cloves
1 teaspoon dried parsley
2 teaspoons grated Parmesan cheese
1 egg
500g/1lb 2oz beef mince
3 large French baguettes or sub rolls, split in half
1 slice of processed cheese (optional)

FOR THE MARINARA SAUCE:
1 tablespoon olive oil
1 garlic clove, finely chopped
1 x 400g tin of chopped tomatoes
1 teaspoon dried Italian herbs
1 teaspoon sugar
1 teaspoon sea salt
Pinch of black pepper

1   Preheat the oven to 180°C/350°F/Gas Mark 4.
2   In a blender, combine the white bread, Italian herbs, garlic, parsley and Parmesan cheese. Add the blended mixture to a large bowl along with the egg and the beef mince. Use your hands to mix thoroughly until well combined.

3   Shape the mince mixture into 10–12 balls and arrange on a baking tray, leaving a little space between each meatball, then place the tray of meatballs on the middle shelf of the oven and cook for around 20 minutes, or until cooked through.

4   Meanwhile, make the marinara sauce. Heat the oil in a pan and fry the garlic on a low heat for 1–2 minutes. Add 50ml/2fl oz water to the pan along with the tinned chopped tomatoes, dried Italian herbs, sugar, sea salt and pepper. Bring the sauce to a boil, then reduce the heat to low and simmer for 15–20 minutes, stirring occasionally.

5   Preheat the grill to high.

6   When the meatballs are cooked, transfer them from the baking tray and into the pan. Mix carefully to coat the meatballs with the marinara sauce.

7   Place 3–4 meatballs into the roll with a little sauce. Add the cheese slice, if using, and place the open sandwich under the hot grill for 2–3 minutes. Repeat the process to make all three sandwiches. Allow the sandwich to rest for 2 minutes and then serve.

Onion Rings (American Fast-food Style)

SERVES 2

4 tablespoons plain flour
2 tablespoons cornflour
½ teaspoon sea salt, plus extra for sprinkling
Pinch of black pepper
2 pinches of bicarbonate of soda (baking soda)
2 tablespoons vegetable oil
350–400ml/12–14fl oz beer or lager
2 large onions, peeled and sliced into rings
Vegetable oil, for deep frying

1   In a large bowl, combine the plain flour, cornflour, sea salt, black
    pepper, bicarbonate of soda, vegetable oil and beer or lager. Mix well
    to create a thin batter with the consistency of single cream.

2   When you're ready to cook the onion rings, set your deep fryer to
    180°C/350°F. Alternatively, fill a wok or large frying pan one third
    full with vegetable oil and heat to 180°C/350°F. The oil is ready
    when a few breadcrumbs dropped into the oil sizzle immediately.
    Dip the onion rings into the batter and allow any excess to drip off.
    Carefully place the onion rings into the hot oil and fry for around
    3–4 minutes, turning occasionally, until golden and crisp.

3   Remove the onion rings using a slotted spoon and drain off any
    excess oil on kitchen paper. Place the onion rings onto greaseproof
    paper, sprinkle with sea salt and allow to stand for 1–2 minutes
    before serving.

Potato Wedges (American Fast-food Style)

Wedges are the ideal accompaniment to pizza and breaded chicken strips; Maris Peer and Maris Piper potatoes provide excellent results in this recipe.

SERVES 1–2

2 potatoes, each cut lengthways into 8 wedges
1 tablespoon olive oil
½ tablespoon plain flour
¼ teaspoon garlic powder
¼ teaspoon onion powder
Sea salt and freshly ground black pepper

1 Preheat the oven to 220°C/425°F/Gas Mark 7.
2 Place the potato wedges in a bowl and add the olive oil, flour, garlic powder and onion powder, then season with a pinch each of salt and pepper. Mix well.
3 Arrange the potato wedges on a lightly greased baking tray and cook in the middle of the oven for 25–30 minutes, turning occasionally, until cooked through and golden. Serve with a selection of dips.

Fully Loaded Baked Potatoes (American Fast-food Style)

It's worth taking the time to bake the potatoes in the oven and to grill the bacon. If time is short, however, you could cook both in a microwave, if you have one.

SERVES 2

2 large baking potatoes
1 teaspoon vegetable oil
Pinch of sea salt
4 slices of bacon
1 tablespoon butter
1 tablespoon single cream
2 handfuls of grated cheese, plus extra for topping
Pinch of paprika powder
2 spring onions, sliced, to decorate
Sea salt and freshly ground black pepper

1   Preheat the oven to 200°C/400°F/Gas Mark 6.
2   Pierce each potato several times with a knife and rub them with vegetable oil and sea salt. Place them directly onto the middle rack of the oven and cook for 1 hour, or until the skin is crisp and the potatoes are soft on the inside.
3   Meanwhile, preheat the grill to medium–high. Grill the bacon slices for 4–6 minutes, turning halfway through cooking, until they turn crispy. Set aside.
4   When they are ready, remove the potatoes from the oven and set them aside to cool for 5 minutes. Slice each potato in half and use a spoon to scoop the flesh out and into a bowl.
5   Add the butter, cream and grated cheese to the potato flesh, season with a pinch each of salt and pepper, and mix well with a fork, mashing the flesh as you go. Spoon the potato mixture back into the potato skins. Grate a little extra cheese over the top, then return the

filled skins to the oven and bake for a further 10–15 minutes until the fillings are piping hot and the cheese on top is golden and crispy.

6   Place the filled potato skins onto a plate or serving dish. Sprinkle with the paprika, then break the bacon into pieces and crumble over the top of the filled skins. Decorate with the sliced spring onions and serve.

Garlic Mushrooms (American Fast-food Style)

SERVES 1–2

120g/4oz plain flour
½ teaspoon sea salt
1 egg
200ml/7fl oz whole milk
6 tablespoons breadcrumbs
¼ teaspoon garlic powder
¼ teaspoon onion powder
¼ teaspoon dried Italian herbs
Pinch of cayenne pepper
Pinch of black pepper
10–12 small button mushrooms
Vegetable oil, for deep frying

1   In a large bowl, combine the plain flour and sea salt and mix well, and in another bowl whisk together the egg and milk to combine thoroughly.

2   In a bowl, combine the breadcrumbs, garlic powder, onion powder, Italian herbs, cayenne pepper and black pepper.

3   Coat each mushroom in the flour mixture and set aside.

4   Add the egg and milk mixture to the flour, then mix well, adding more milk if necessary, until you have a medium–thick batter.

5   Keeping one hand dry, dip the floured mushrooms first into the batter and then into the breadcrumbs. Repeat to coat all of the mushrooms in breadcrumbs.

6   When you're ready to cook the mushrooms, set your deep fryer to 180°C/350°F. Alternatively, fill a wok or large frying pan one third full with vegetable oil and heat to 180°C/350°F. The oil is ready when a few breadcrumbs dropped into the oil sizzle immediately. Add the mushrooms and deep-fry over a medium heat for around

2–3 minutes or until golden. Once cooked, remove the mushrooms from the pan and drain off any excess oil. Serve with Garlic Kebab Sauce (see p.99).

Fried Pickles (American Fast-food Style)

SERVES 2

4 heaped tablespoons plain flour
2 heaped tablespoons cornflour
½ teaspoon sea salt, plus extra for sprinkling
Pinch of black pepper
2 pinches of bicarbonate of soda
2 tablespoons vegetable oil, plus extra for deep frying
350–400ml/12–14fl oz beer or lager
1–2 dill pickles, sliced

1   In a large bowl, combine the plain flour, cornflour, sea salt, black pepper, bicarbonate of soda, vegetable oil and beer or lager. Mix well until you have a thin batter, the consistency of single cream.

2   When you're ready to cook the pickles, set your deep fryer to 180°C/350°F. Alternatively, fill a wok or large frying pan one third full with vegetable oil and heat to 180°C/350°F. The oil is ready when a few breadcrumbs dropped into the oil sizzle immediately.

3   Dip the pickle slices into the batter and allow any excess to drip off. Carefully place the pickle slices into the hot oil and fry for around 3–4 minutes, turning occasionally, until they are cooked through, golden and crisp.

4   Use a slotted spoon to remove the pickles from the oil. Drain off any excess oil on kitchen paper, and place the pickles on greaseproof paper. Sprinkle with sea salt and allow to stand for 1–2 minutes before serving with ketchup or dips.

Corn on the Cob (American Fast-food Style)

These smoky roasted corn cobs are a delicious accompaniment to any fried-chicken dish. For added flavour, sprinkle a little cayenne pepper, garlic powder, ground cumin or smoked paprika over the cooked corn.

SERVES 2

4 teaspoons butter at room temperature, plus extra to serve (optional)

2 corn cobs, husks removed

Sea salt and freshly ground black pepper

1   Preheat the oven to 220°C/425°F/Gas Mark 7.

2   Soften the butter slightly with a teaspoon and lay out two tin-foil sheets, each large enough to wrap a corn cob. Smother one corn cob with 1 teaspoon of the softened butter, then wrap the foil around the cob and seal tightly. Repeat with the other corn cob.

3   Place the wrapped cobs on a baking tray and place in the oven for about 20 minutes. Open the foil, add half the remaining butter to each corn cob and cook uncovered for a further 15–20 minutes, or until the corn cobs take on a little colour.

4   Remove the cooked corn cobs from the oven and cover with more softened butter, if using. Season generously with sea salt and pepper and serve hot.

Mac 'n' Cheese Bites (American Fast-food Style)

Although these bites are undoubtedly the ultimate way to use leftovers, the truth is they're so good you'll whip up a batch of mac 'n' cheese with the sole intention of making these.

SERVES 1–2

4 tablespoons plain flour

1 egg

50ml/1½fl oz semi-skimmed milk

6 tablespoons panko breadcrumbs

¼ teaspoon garlic powder

¼ teaspoon onion powder

½ teaspoon dried Italian herbs

Pinch of cayenne pepper

5–6 tablespoons cooked, cooled and chilled Mac 'n' Cheese (see p.61)

Vegetable oil, for deep frying

Salt and freshly ground black pepper

1   Season the flour in a bowl with a little sea salt and pepper, then tip it onto a plate and spread into an even layer.

2   In a separate small bowl, combine the egg and milk and mix thoroughly.

3   In a large bowl, combine the panko breadcrumbs, garlic powder, onion powder, dried Italian herbs and cayenne pepper, and season with a pinch each of sea salt and black pepper.

4   Using lightly floured hands, work with around 1 tablespoon of cooked and cooled mac 'n' cheese at a time. Keeping one hand dry, dip the tablespoon of mac 'n' cheese first into the plain flour, then into the egg and milk mixture, and finally into the seasoned breadcrumbs. Repeat the process until you have breaded all of the bites.

5   When you're ready to cook the bites, set your deep fryer to 180°C/350°F. Alternatively, fill a wok or large frying pan one third full with vegetable oil and heat to 180°C/350°F. The oil is ready when a few breadcrumbs dropped into the oil sizzle immediately. Carefully place the mac 'n' cheese bites into the oil and fry for around 2–3 minutes, until golden. Remove the bites from the oil using a slotted spoon and drain off any excess oil on kitchen paper. Allow to stand for 1–2 minutes before serving.

Hamburger (American Fast-food Style)

SERVES 1

About 55g/2oz beef mince (minimum 20% fat)
1 burger bun, halved
½ tablespoon tomato ketchup
1 teaspoon yellow mustard
1 teaspoon finely chopped onion
2 thin slices of gherkin
1 slice of processed cheese (optional)
Sea salt and freshly ground black pepper

1   Preheat the oven to its lowest setting.

2   Roll the beef mince into a ball. Lay out a sheet of greaseproof paper, place the ball of mince on top and lay over another sheet, then flatten the mince between the sheets into a thin, circular patty, slightly bigger than the size of your burger bun. Cover and place in the coldest part of the fridge for 1–2 hours.

3   Place a dry frying pan over a medium heat. Toast the burger-bun halves, cut-sides down, in the pan for about 30 seconds or until toasted and golden. Remove the bun halves from the pan and set aside.

4   Place the burger patty onto the hot dry pan and cook for 60–90 seconds; apply very gentle pressure with a spatula to ensure even browning. Flip the burger, sprinkle over a pinch each of sea salt and pepper and cook for a further 60 seconds, or until cooked through and juices run clear. Remove from the heat and set aside.

5   Place five dots of ketchup on the inside of the bun lid, positioning the dots like the '5' on a dice. Add five smaller drops of yellow mustard between the ketchup dots. Add a pinch of finely chopped onion , the two gherkin slices, and the slice of cheese, if using. Finally, top with the burger patty and finish off with the bun bottom.

6 Wrap the burger in foil or baking paper, invert so that the bun lid is at the top, and place in the oven for 3–4 minutes to heat through and allow the flavours to combine. Serve with French fries.

Quarter Pounder Burger (American Fast-food Style)

SERVES 1

About 115g/4oz beef mince (minimum 20% fat)
1 large burger bun, halved
1 tablespoon tomato ketchup
2 teaspoons yellow mustard
1 tablespoon finely chopped onion
4 thin slices of gherkin
1 slice of processed cheese (optional)
Sea salt and freshly ground black pepper

1 Preheat the oven to its lowest setting.
2 Roll the beef mince into a ball. Lay out a sheet of greaseproof paper, place the ball of mince on top and lay over another sheet, then flatten the mince between the sheets into a thin circular patty, slightly bigger than the size of your burger bun. Cover and place in the coldest part of the fridge for 1–2 hours.
3 Heat a dry frying pan over a medium–high heat. Toast the burger-bun halves cut-side down in the pan for around 30 seconds or until golden. Remove them from the pan and set aside.
4 Place the burger patty onto the hot, dry pan and cook for 2–3 minutes. Apply very gentle pressure with a spatula to ensure even browning.
5 Flip the burger, season with a pinch each of sea salt and black pepper and cook for a further 2 minutes, or until cooked through and juices run clear.
6 Place five dots of ketchup on the inside of the bun lid, positioning the dots like the '5' on a dice. Add five smaller drops of yellow mustard between the ketchup dots. Add a pinch of finely chopped onion , the two gherkin slices, and the slice of cheese, if using. Finally, top with the burger patty and finish off with the bun bottom.

7 Wrap the burger in foil or baking paper, invert so that the bun lid is at the top, and place in the oven for 3–4 minutes to heat through and allow the flavours to combine. Serve with French fries.

Mega Burger with Special Burger Sauce (American Fast-food Style)

This classic burger has an added bread layer in the middle and two burger patties, served with a Special Burger Sauce. You can use the sauce on hot dogs or as a sandwich dressing too.

SERVES 1

About 115g/4oz beef mince (minimum 20% fat)
1 burger bun, halved, and 1 bottom half burger bun
2 tablespoons Special Burger Sauce (see below)
2 teaspoons finely chopped onion
1 small handful of shredded iceberg lettuce
4 thin slices of gherkin
1 slice of processed cheese
Sea salt and freshly ground black pepper

FOR THE SPECIAL BURGER SAUCE
(ENOUGH FOR 3 MEGA BURGERS):
4 tablespoons mayonnaise
2 teaspoons yellow mustard
2 teaspoons tomato ketchup
1 tablespoon finely chopped gherkin

1   First, make the Special Burger Sauce. In a small bowl, combine the mayonnaise, yellow mustard and ketchup. Add the chopped gherkin and mix well. Refrigerate for at least 1 hour before using. (Any leftover will keep in the fridge for 2–3 days.)
2   Preheat the oven to its lowest setting.
3   Halve the mince and roll each half into a ball. Lay out a sheet of greaseproof paper, place the balls of mince on top and lay over another sheet, then flatten the mince between the sheets into thin circular patties, slightly bigger than the size of your burger bun. Cover and place in the coldest part of the fridge for 1–2 hours.

4   Heat a dry frying pan on a medium–high heat. Toast the burger-bun halves cut-sides down in the pan for around 30 seconds or until golden and toasted. Remove from the pan and set aside.

5   Place the burger patties onto the hot dry pan and cook for 2 minutes; apply very gentle pressure with a spatula to ensure even browning. Flip the burgers, season with a pinch each of sea salt and black pepper and cook for a further 2 minutes, or until cooked through and the juices run clear. (If necessary, cook the burgers one at a time and keep warm in the oven at the lowest available setting until required.)

6   Dress the bottom- and middle-layer bun halves with 1 tablespoon of Special Burger Sauce each. Add a teaspoon of finely chopped onion and a handful of shredded iceberg lettuce. On the middle bun half, place four gherkin slices. On the bottom bun half, add the processed cheese slice.

7   Place the burger patties onto the dressed buns. Carefully lift the middle layer and place it on top of the bottom layer. Add the top bun half.

8   Wrap the burger loosely in foil or baking paper and place in the oven for 3–4 minutes to heat through and allow the flavours to combine. Serve with French fries.

Whopping Big Burger (American Fast-food Style)

It's all in the assembly when it comes to this classic burger, fit for a king!

SERVES 1

Roughly 113 g/4oz beef mince (minimum 20% fat)

1 large sesame seed burger bun

1 tablespoon mayonnaise

1 small handful of shredded iceberg lettuce

1 tablespoon tomato ketchup

4 thin slices of gherkin

2 raw onion ring slices

2 tomato slices

Pinch of salt and pinch of black pepper

1   Roll the beef mince into a ball. Using a sheet of greaseproof paper, flatten the mince into a thin, circular patty, slightly bigger than the size of your burger bun. Cover and place in the coldest part of the fridge for 1–2 hours. The burger patty may also be frozen if desired.

2   Heat a griddle pan to a medium-high heat. Toast the burger buns face down in the pan for around 30 seconds or until golden. Set aside.

3   Place the burger patty onto the hot, dry griddle pan and cook for 2–3 minutes. Apply very gentle pressure with a spatula to ensure even browning. Flip the burger. Add a pinch of salt and pepper and cook for a further 2 minutes or until cooked through and juices run clear.

4   Spread the mayonnaise on the top burger bun and add the shredded lettuce. Place the burger patty onto the bottom bun and dress with the tomato ketchup, gherkin slices, raw onion ring slices and tomato slices.

5 Place the top bun on top of the dressed bottom bun. Wrap the burger loosely in foil or baking paper and place in the oven at the lowest available setting for 3–4 minutes to combine flavours and heat through. Serve with French fries.

BBQ Pork Burger (American Fast-food Style)

This cult classic sandwich is a limited-edition menu item, now available in your home all year round! Using a ridged griddle pan when forming the burger patty helps to imitate the 'rib' effect used by fast-food chains.

SERVES 1

About 55g/2oz pork mince
Pinch of white sugar
1 burger bun, halved
2 tablespoons barbecue sauce, plus extra to serve (optional)
1 teaspoon vegetable oil
½ small onion, finely sliced
4 thin slices of gherkin
Sea salt and freshly ground black pepper

1   Preheat the oven to its lowest setting.
2   Put the mince and sugar in a bowl and season with a pinch each of sea salt and pepper. Using slightly wet hands, mix thoroughly and roll the mixture into a ball.
3   Lay a sheet of greaseproof paper over a ridged griddle pan. Flatten the mixture on the paper into a thin circular patty, slightly bigger than the size of the burger bun. Carefully remove the patty and paper and place in the freezer for at least 1 hour. (You can leave it frozen for up to 1 month, and you can cook from frozen.)
4   When you're ready to cook, heat a dry frying pan on a medium heat. Toast the burger-bun halves cut-sides down for 30 seconds, or until golden and toasted. Remove from the heat and allow to cool slightly.
5   Spread 1 tablespoon of barbecue sauce on the bottom bun half.
6   Heat the oil in a frying pan over a low–medium heat. Add the frozen pork patty and cook for 5–6 minutes or until just cooked through,

turning occasionally and applying gentle pressure to ensure even browning.

7   Just before the patty is cooked, brush generously with the remaining barbecue sauce on both sides and allow to cook for a further 30 seconds.

8   Place the cooked pork patty on the bottom bun half. Top with the finely sliced onion and gherkin slices and add a little more barbecue sauce, if using. Add the bun lid and wrap the burger in foil or baking paper.

9   Place the wrapped burger in the oven at the lowest available setting for 2–3 minutes to heat through and allow the flavours to combine. Serve with French fries.

Philly Cheesesteak
(American Fast-food Style)

The key to this sandwich is to ensure the steak is sliced as thinly as possible, enabling extremely quick cooking and juicy, tender steak pieces for your finished sandwich. US customers often include 'cheeze whiz', a processed cheese product. Provolone or even mozzarella cheese will also work well. There is fierce debate over which type of cheese is the right type, so feel free to use your favourite. Optional additions to this sandwich include green peppers, mushrooms, chilli sauce, pizza sauce or mayonnaise.

SERVES 1

About 115g/4oz sirloin beef steak, sliced into thin strips
2 tablespoons vegetable oil
1 onion, thinly sliced
1 sub roll, hot dog roll or small French baguette, sliced open
1 slice of processed cheese
Ketchup or yellow mustard, to serve (optional)
Sea salt and freshly ground black pepper

1 Preheat the oven to 120°C/245°F/Gas Mark ½.
2 Place the steak strips in a bowl with 1 tablespoon of the vegetable oil and stir to coat.
3 Heat the remaining oil in a frying pan on a medium heat. Add the sliced onion to the pan and cook for 8–10 minutes, until the onion begins to darken and become crisp.
4 Increase the heat to high and add the steak. Season with a little sea salt and pepper, then stir-fry for 2–3 minutes or until the steak is just cooked through.
5 Fill the roll with the cooked onion and steak. Cut the processed cheese slice into strips and add to the roll.

6 Place in a warm oven for 3–4 minutes to allow the cheese to melt. Then serve straightaway with ketchup or yellow mustard, if you wish.

Chicken Fillet Burger
(American Fast-food Style)

SERVES 1

1 tablespoon vegetable oil

100ml/3½fl oz water

3 tablespoons tomato ketchup

½ teaspoon dried Italian herbs

¼ teaspoon paprika

Pinch of onion powder

¼ teaspoon liquid smoke (optional, but recommended)

1 small skinless, boneless chicken breast fillet (about 85g/3oz weight)

1 burger bun, halved

1 tablespoon mayonnaise

1 handful of shredded lettuce

2 large tomato slices

Sea salt and freshly ground black pepper

1   In a bowl or food-safe bag, combine the vegetable oil, water, tomato ketchup, Italian herbs, paprika, onion powder and liquid smoke (if using) and season with a pinch each of sea salt and pepper.

2   Using a meat mallet, pound the chicken breast fillet until thin, then use scissors to shape the chicken piece to your burger bun. Add the chicken piece to the bowl or food bag and marinate in the fridge for at least 4 hours, or overnight if possible.

3   When you're ready to cook, heat a griddle pan on a medium–high heat. Toast the bun halves cut-side down on the griddle pan for about 30 seconds or until golden and toasted. Remove from the pan and set aside.

4   Place the marinated chicken onto the hot griddle pan. Cook for 3–4 minutes, then flip the chicken piece and continue to cook for another 3–4 minutes or until the chicken is cooked through.

5 Dress the bun lid with mayonnaise, shredded lettuce and
   tomato slices. Place the cooked chicken piece on top, then add
   the bun bottom, invert and serve straightaway with French
   fries.

Chicken Sandwich Burger (American Fast-food Style)

SERVES 1

120g/4oz plain flour
1 teaspoon onion powder
½ teaspoon garlic powder
1 teaspoon sea salt
½ teaspoon black pepper
1 egg
120ml/4fl oz whole milk
1 small skinless, boneless chicken breast fillet (about 85g/3oz weight)
1 burger bun, halved
Vegetable oil, for deep frying
Pinch of onion powder
1 tablespoon mayonnaise
Handful of shredded lettuce

1   In a bowl, combine the plain flour, onion powder, garlic powder, sea salt and black pepper. In a separate bowl, combine the egg and milk.
2   Trim any excess fat from the chicken breast fillet, then using a meat mallet, pound the fillet until thin. Use scissors to shape the chicken piece to fit the burger bun.
3   Keeping one hand dry, dip the shaped chicken piece first into the seasoned flour, then into the egg and milk mixture, and finally into the seasoned flour once again. Leave to rest for a few minutes and repeat – dipping the shaped, coated breast in flour, egg/milk and flour.
4   Heat a dry frying pan on a medium heat. Toast the burger-bun halves cut-sides down in the pan for around 30 seconds or until golden. Remove from the pan and set aside.
5   Half-fill a saucepan with vegetable oil and heat to 180°C/350°F. The oil is ready when breadcrumbs dropped into the oil sizzle as

they hit the liquid. Deep-fry the chicken burger in the hot oil on a medium heat for about 5–6 minutes, or until the chicken is golden brown and cooked through. Remove the chicken from the pan using a slotted spoon and drain off any excess oil on kitchen paper.

6 Add the onion powder to the mayonnaise and stir through to combine. Dress the bun lid with the flavoured mayonnaise, then the shredded lettuce. Place the cooked chicken piece on top. Finish off with the bun bottom, invert and serve immediately with French fries.

Fish Fillet Burger
(American Fast-food Style)

Hoki was the traditional choice of fish fillet for sandwiches
for many years in American restaurants, but recently Alaskan
pollock has become more widely used. Any firm white fish will
provide good results.

3–4 tablespoons plain flour
¼ teaspoon sea salt
¼ teaspoon black pepper
1 egg
6 tablespoons whole milk
6 tablespoons breadcrumbs
1 small white fish fillet
2–3 tablespoons vegetable oil
1 burger bun, halved
1 tablespoon tartare sauce
½ slice of processed cheese

1   In a bowl combine the plain flour, sea salt and black pepper. In a
    separate bowl, whisk the egg and milk together thoroughly to
    combine.
2   Pour the breadcrumbs into a bowl and set aside.
3   Trim the fish fillet to fit the burger bun, then, keeping one hand dry,
    dip the fish fillet first into the seasoned flour, then into the egg and
    milk mixture, and finally into the breadcrumbs.
4   Cover and set the breaded fish aside in the fridge for 1 hour. This
    will help the breadcrumb coating to stick to the fish.
5   When you are ready to cook, heat a dry frying pan on a medium
    heat. Toast the bun halves face down in the pan for around 30
    seconds, or until golden and toasted. Remove from the pan and set
    aside.
6   Heat the oil in the frying pan and fry the breaded fish fillet on a

medium heat for around 5–6 minutes or until golden and cooked through. Turn the fish once during cooking.

7   Dress the bun lid with the tartare sauce. Add the cooked fish and place the cheese slice on top. Finish off with the bun bottom, invert and serve immediately with French fries.

...ern Fried Chicken with Fresh ...oleslaw (American Fast-food Style)

Made fresh within an hour or so of serving, the simple coleslaw recipe that comes with this chicken offers everything a good coleslaw should! For a spicy fried chicken, mix 1 tablespoon of your favourite hot sauce into the egg, milk and water mixture before breading the chicken.

SERVES 1–2

120g/4oz plain flour
1½ teaspoons garlic powder
½ teaspoon onion powder
1 teaspoon paprika
½ teaspoon cayenne pepper
½ teaspoon dried Italian herbs
1 teaspoon sea salt
½ teaspoon black pepper
1 egg
100ml/3½fl oz whole milk
6 chicken pieces (thighs and drumsticks)
Vegetable oil, for deep frying

FOR THE COLESLAW:
¼ small onion, finely chopped
¼ head of white cabbage (roughly 200g/8oz), finely sliced
2 carrots, grated
2–3 tablespoons mayonnaise

1 First, make the coleslaw. In a bowl, combine the onion, white cabbage and carrot. Add the mayonnaise to taste and mix thoroughly again. Refrigerate for 1 hour before using.

2 To make the chicken, in a large bowl or food-safe bag, combine the plain flour, garlic powder, onion powder, paprika, cayenne

pepper, Italian herbs, sea salt and black pepper. Mix well to fully combine.

3 In a separate bowl, combine the egg and milk with 50ml/2fl oz of water and whisk thoroughly until well combined.

4 Keeping one hand dry, dip the chicken pieces first into the seasoned flour, then into the egg, milk and water mixture, and finally into the seasoned flour again. Repeat, until you have coated all the chicken pieces twice in the seasoned flour.

5 When you're ready to cook the chicken, set your deep fryer to 180°C/350°F. Alternatively, fill a wok or large frying pan one third full with vegetable oil and heat to 180°C/350°F. The oil is ready when a few breadcrumbs dropped into the oil sizzle immediately. Deep-fry the chicken pieces in the hot oil for about 7–8 minutes. Turn the chicken pieces and cook for a further 5–6 minutes or until the chicken is cooked through, crispy and golden.

6 Remove the chicken pieces from the pan using a slotted spoon and drain off any excess oil on kitchen paper. Serve straightaway with the coleslaw alongside.

NOTE: If you're cooking for several people, fry the chicken in batches and keep it warm in an oven on its lowest possible setting.

Buffalo Wings (American Fast-food Style)

These classic wings are named after their city of origin: Buffalo, New York State. The fried wings are tossed in a butter-based hot sauce and served with celery sticks and blue cheese dip. Many takeaway restaurants in the USA now also offer 'boneless wings'. These are made not from wings but from boneless chicken breast fillets, breaded and fried, and coated in the classic Buffalo hot sauce.

SERVES 1–2

120g/4oz plain flour
½ teaspoon paprika
¼ teaspoon cayenne pepper
¼ teaspoon sea salt
4 tablespoons butter
4 tablespoons hot pepper sauce
¼ teaspoon garlic powder
6 chicken wings, split into 12 wing pieces and tips discarded
Vegetable oil, for deep frying

1   In a large bowl, combine the plain flour, paprika, cayenne pepper and sea salt. Set aside.
2   Place a small pan over a low heat and add the butter, hot pepper sauce and garlic powder, stirring to combine until the butter has melted. Mix well.
3   Toss the chicken wing pieces in the bowl of seasoned flour. When you're ready to cook the wings, set your deep fryer to 180°C/350°F. Alternatively, fill a wok or large frying pan one third full with vegetable oil and heat to 180°C/350°F. The oil is ready when a few breadcrumbs dropped into the oil sizzle immediately. Deep-fry the chicken pieces in the hot oil on a medium heat for around 8–10 minutes, or until the chicken is cooked through and golden.

4 Once cooked, remove the chicken pieces from the pan and drain off any excess oil on kitchen paper. Dip each wing piece into the prepared sauce until well coated.

5 Arrange the Buffalo wings on a plate or serving dish. Serve with celery sticks and Blue Cheese dip (see p.49).

Honey BBQ Chicken Wings (American Fast-food Style)

SERVES 1–2

6 tablespoons tomato ketchup

1 teaspoon white vinegar

2 tablespoons soy sauce

2 tablespoons Worcestershire sauce

1 teaspoon Tabasco sauce

1 teaspoon Dijon mustard

2 tablespoons honey

1 teaspoon garlic powder

½ tablespoon smoked paprika

¼ teaspoon black pepper

2 tablespoons vegetable oil

6 chicken wings, split into 12 wing pieces, tips discarded

Lemon slices, to decorate

1   Make a marinade by combining the tomato ketchup, white vinegar, soy sauce, Worcestershire sauce, Tabasco sauce, Dijon mustard, honey, garlic powder, smoked paprika and black pepper with 4 tablespoons of water in a bowl. Reserve 2 tablespoons of the marinade in a separate bowl for basting, if you like.

2   Add the vegetable oil and the chicken wing pieces to the remaining marinade and rub the marinade thoroughly into each chicken wing piece. Cover the bowl and refrigerate for at least 4 hours, or over-night if possible.

3   Preheat the oven to 200°C/400°F/Gas Mark 6.

4   Remove the chicken wings from the fridge and arrange them on a wire rack over a baking tray. Bake in the middle of the oven for 15 minutes, then turn the chicken pieces and cook for a further 15 minutes, then baste with the reserved marinade (if using) and turn the chicken pieces once again.

5 Move the baking tray to the top shelf of the oven and cook for a further 5–6 minutes, then baste once more, turn the chicken pieces for a final time and return to the top of the oven for a further 5–6 minutes, or until the pieces are cooked through.

6 Remove the chicken wings from the oven and arrange on a plate or serving dish. Serve decorated with a few slices of lemon.

Boneless Buffalo Chicken Strips (American Fast-food Style)

Hot and fiery, these 'boneless wings' are the latest and spiciest addition to US fast-food menus.

SERVES 1

4 tablespoons plain flour
6 tablespoons panko breadcrumbs
¼ teaspoon garlic powder
¼ teaspoon onion powder
½ teaspoon dried Italian herbs
Pinch of black pepper
1 egg
120ml/4fl oz semi-skimmed milk
1 large skinless, boneless chicken breast fillet (about 115g/4 oz weight)
Vegetable oil, for deep frying
2 tablespoons hot pepper sauce
2 tablespoons butter

1   Spread the plain flour over a plate. Set aside.
2   In a large bowl, combine the panko breadcrumbs, garlic powder, onion powder, dried Italian herbs and black pepper. Set aside.
3   In a small bowl, combine the egg and milk and mix thoroughly.
4   Trim any excess fat from the chicken breast and cut into 5–6 long strips.
5   Keeping one hand dry, dip the chicken strips first into the plain flour, then into the egg and milk mixture, and finally into the seasoned breadcrumbs.
6   When you're ready to cook the chicken strips, set your deep fryer to 180°C/350°F. Alternatively, fill a wok or large frying pan one third full with vegetable oil and heat to 180°C/350°F. The oil is ready when a few breadcrumbs dropped into the oil sizzle immediately.

Carefully place the breaded chicken pieces into the oil over a medium–high heat and fry for 2 minutes. Remove the chicken pieces from the pan and set aside on a plate for 1 minute. This will allow the chicken to continue cooking inside without overcooking the breaded coating.

7   Return the chicken pieces to the oil and fry for a further 2 minutes or until the breadcrumbs begin to turn golden and the chicken is cooked through. Remove the chicken strips from the pan using a slotted spoon and drain off any excess oil on kitchen paper.

8   Place a small pan over a low heat and add the hot pepper sauce and butter. Combine well into a glossy sauce and continue to heat until piping hot.

9   Place the cooked chicken strips into a sealable container. Add the hot sauce, close the lid and shake the container well until all of the chicken pieces are fully coated. Serve with celery, Blue Cheese dip (see p.49) or coleslaw.

Dips (American Fast-food Style)
SOURED CREAM AND CHIVE

This cooling dip is perfect during summer weather, adding a refreshing angle to baked potatoes or any barbecue food.

SERVES 1–2
4 tablespoons soured cream
4 tablespoons soft cheese
1 garlic clove, crushed
About 1 tablespoon of finely snipped chives
Pinch of paprika or cayenne pepper (optional)
Sea salt

1   In a bowl, combine the soured cream, soft cheese, crushed garlic and chives, and season with a pinch of sea salt. Add the paprika or cayenne pepper, if using.
2   Mix thoroughly and refrigerate for at least 1 hour before serving with tortilla chips, breadsticks or fresh vegetables.

GARLIC & HERB

SERVES 1
2 tablespoons mayonnaise
½ teaspoon American mustard
¼ teaspoon garlic powder
¼ teaspoon dried parsley
2–3 tablespoons semi-skimmed milk

1   In a small bowl, combine the mayonnaise, American mustard, garlic powder and dried parsley. Mix well.
2   Slowly add the semi-skimmed milk and mix thoroughly until the sauce reaches the desired consistency. Serve with pizzas and kebabs.

BLUE CHEESE

SERVES 1–2
About 50g/2oz Stilton cheese
75ml/2½fl oz soured cream
1 tablespoon mayonnaise
1 teaspoon lemon juice
Sea salt and freshly ground black pepper

1   In a large bowl, combine the Stilton, soured cream and mayonnaise. Mix thoroughly until soft and smooth.
2   Add the lemon juice, and season with a pinch each of sea salt and pepper.
3   Mix thoroughly once more, then chill the blue cheese dip in the fridge for at least 2 hours before serving with Boneless Buffalo Chicken Strips (see p.46).

TARTARE SAUCE

SERVES 3–4
120ml/4fl oz mayonnaise
1 teaspoon lemon juice
1 teaspoon finely chopped onion
2 tablespoons finely chopped gherkin

1   In a bowl, combine the mayonnaise, lemon juice, chopped onion and gherkin. Mix well and refrigerate for at least 2 hours before using.
2   Serve with any seafood, or use to dress Fish Fillet Burgers (see p.38).

HONEY MUSTARD

SERVES 1–2

60ml/2fl oz water
1 teaspoon cornflour
2 tablespoons honey
½ tablespoon lemon juice
2 teaspoons Dijon mustard
¼ teaspoon onion powder

1   In a small pan, combine the water and cornflour. Mix well, add the honey and bring the mixture to the boil, stirring frequently.
2   Remove the pan from the heat. Add the lemon juice, mustard and onion powder and mix well again.
3   Pour the dip into a bowl and refrigerate until needed. Serve with Southern Fried Chicken (see p.40).

American BBQ Ribs
(American Fast-food Style)

SERVES 1–2

800g/2 lb pork ribs
2 tablespoons red wine vinegar
6 tablespoons tomato ketchup
1½ tablespoons white wine vinegar
2 tablespoons Worcestershire sauce
1 tablespoon American mustard
1 tablespoon margarine
1 tablespoon treacle
½ teaspoon Tabasco sauce
1 teaspoon vegetable oil
Sea salt

1 Preheat the oven to 180°C/350°F/Gas Mark 4. Arrange the ribs on a
   large deep roasting tray.
2 In a small bowl, mix the red wine vinegar with 2 tablespoons of
   water and pour the mixture over the pork ribs.
3 Cover the roasting tray loosely with foil and bake the ribs in the
   oven for about 40 minutes, until cooked. Remove the ribs from
   the oven and arrange on a plate to cool. At this point you can
   finish the ribs immediately, or refrigerate them and continue the
   next day.
4 Make the barbecue sauce. In a bowl, combine the tomato ketchup
   white wine vinegar, Worcestershire sauce, American mustard,
   margarine, treacle, Tabasco sauce and vegetable oil with
   2 tablespoons of water. Season with a pinch of sea salt and mix
   thoroughly.
5 Heat a dry griddle pan on a low–medium heat. Tip the cooked ribs
   into a large bowl and add 2 tablespoons of the prepared barbecue
   sauce. Use your hands to mix thoroughly, coating the ribs, then
   place them on the griddle pan.

6 Cook the ribs, turning occasionally, for 10–12 minutes, basting with the remaining barbecue sauce every few minutes, until the sauce caramelises. Serve with sweetcorn and coleslaw.

BBQ Pulled Pork (American Fast-food Style)

Smothered in a barbecue sauce made with its own juices, this juicy pork is perfect inside a burger bun or a wrap. Although marinating and baking requires some time, the preparation is easy and once in the oven the pork can be left unattended while cooking.

1 teaspoon dried coriander leaves
2 teaspoons garlic powder
½ teaspoon ground ginger
1 tablespoon paprika
1 tablespoon smoked paprika
1 teaspoon chilli powder
½ teaspoon ground cinnamon
4 tablespoons demerara sugar
2 teaspoons sea salt
½ teaspoon black pepper
½ teaspoon white pepper
1.3kg/3lb skinless, boneless pork shoulder
500ml/18fl oz apple cider
2 teaspoons lemon juice
1 tablespoon honey
1 tablespoon barbecue sauce

1   In a bowl, combine the dried coriander leaves, garlic powder, ground ginger, paprika, smoked paprika, chilli powder, ground cinnamon, 3 tablespoons of the demerara sugar, and the sea salt, black pepper and white pepper. Mix thoroughly and set aside.

2   Trim any excess fat from the pork shoulder, leaving a thin layer for flavour. Wash the pork shoulder and pat it dry with kitchen paper. Using a fork, stab the meat randomly all over. Rub the prepared spice mixture into the pork until completely coated. Place the

marinated meat in a large bowl, cover with cling film and place in the fridge for at least 2 hours, or overnight if possible.

3   Preheat the oven to 150°C/300°F/Gas Mark 2.

4   Arrange a wire rack over a roasting tray. Pour the apple cider into the roasting tray and arrange the pork on the wire rack above. Cover the roasting tin and wire rack with foil. Place in the oven on the middle shelf and bake for 4–5 hours, until the pork has released its juices.

5   Remove the pork from the oven and pour the cooking juices from the roasting tray into a large pan. Scrape the tray well with a spatula to ensure you collect all the meat juices you can. Clean out the roasting tray (or use a second tray) and once again place the meat over the tray on a wire rack.

6   Increase the oven temperature to 200°C/400°F/Gas Mark 6. Return the pork to the oven and cook for a further 30–40 minutes, until the meat is cooked through.

7   Meanwhile, heat the pan of juices on a low heat for 2–3 minutes. Add the remaining 1 tablespoon of demerara sugar and the lemon juice. Mix well, add the honey and barbecue sauce and simmer until thick.

8   When the meat is cooked, remove it from the oven and set aside to cool for 5 minutes. Using two forks (or by hand), shred the pork.

9   Add the shredded pork to the pot and continue simmering until the mixture becomes thick and syrupy. Serve the pulled pork in toasted burger buns, tortilla wraps or tacos with fresh coleslaw (see p.40). Leftover pulled pork will freeze well for up to 1 month.

Barbecue Pulled Chicken (American Fast-food Style)

This spicy, smoky barbecue chicken is a great alternative to pulled pork when time is short. If using stock cubes, dilute with twice as much water as indicated on the packaging, to create a lighter stock.

SERVES 3–4

1 teaspoon garlic powder
½ teaspoon onion powder
¼ teaspoon ground ginger
½ teaspoon smoked paprika
½ teaspoon chilli powder
1 tablespoon brown sugar
¾ teaspoon sea salt
½ teaspoon black pepper
Pinch of white pepper
Pinch of cinnamon
6 skinless, boneless chicken thigh fillets
1 tablespoon vegetable oil
100ml/3½fl oz light chicken stock
2–3 tablespoons barbecue sauce
1 teaspoon Frank's RedHot Sauce (optional, but recommended)

1 In a large bowl, make a dry rub by combining the garlic powder, onion powder, ground ginger, smoked paprika, chilli powder, brown sugar, sea salt, black pepper, white pepper and cinnamon. Mix well.

2 Unfold the chicken thigh fillets and add them to the bowl with the dry rub. Massage the spices into the meat until thoroughly coated. Cover and set aside in the fridge until ready for use. (You can refrigerate the rubbed chicken for 24 hours for a fuller flavour, but the spice mix will give good results even after just 20–30 minutes.)

3 Remove the chicken from the fridge 10 minutes before you're ready to cook.

4 Heat the vegetable oil in a frying pan over a high heat. Place the chicken thighs in the pan and cook without touching them for 2–3 minutes until well browned on one side. Turn the chicken pieces and cook for a further 2–3 minutes until well browned all over.

5 Add the chicken stock, reduce the heat to low and cover with a lid. Simmer the chicken for 10–12 minutes or until the chicken is just cooked through.

6 Remove the lid and use tongs to transfer the chicken thigh fillets to a large plate. Allow the stock to continue simmering over a medium heat with the lid off, so that it reduces, while you 'pull', or shred, the chicken. You can do this using two forks, a knife and fork, or a pair of scissors.

7 Return the shredded chicken to the reduced stock, add the barbecue sauce and Frank's RedHot Sauce, if using. Mix well, cover and simmer the chicken for a further 10 minutes over a low heat until the sauce thickens and the chicken is coated in a rich, sticky sauce.

8 Serve the pulled chicken in toasted burger buns, tortilla wraps or tacos with fresh coleslaw (see p.40). Leftover pulled chicken will freeze well for up to 1 month.

Chilli Con Carne
(American Fast-food Style)

Adding chocolate to a savoury dish may seem strange at first, but is guaranteed to give a smooth, sweet finish to the chilli. A teaspoon of sugar will also work well, should chocolate not be available. The saying goes, 'If you know beans about chilli, you know chilli ain't got no beans!' While this is undoubtedly true in the traditional sense, most modern takeaway and restaurant chilli dishes do include kidney beans.

SERVES 6–8

1 tablespoon vegetable oil
2 large onions, finely chopped
2 red peppers, finely chopped
4 garlic cloves, crushed
1½ teaspoons ground cumin
1 teaspoon ground coriander
2 teaspoons chilli powder
2 teaspoons paprika
1kg/2¼lb beef mince
2 tablespoons tomato purée
1 tablespoon Worcestershire sauce
2 x 400g/14oz tins chopped tomatoes
700ml/25fl oz beef stock (or 700ml/25fl oz boiling water mixed
      with 1½ beef stock cubes)
1 teaspoon dried oregano
1 cinnamon stick
¼ teaspoon black pepper
2 x 400g/14oz tins kidney beans, rinsed and drained
2 squares (around 20g/1oz) of good-quality dark chocolate
      (minimum 60% cocoa solids)

1   Heat the oil in a large stockpot over a low–medium heat. Add the chopped onions and stir-fry for 2–3 minutes, until slightly softened, then add the chopped peppers and crushed garlic. Stir-fry for a further 2 minutes.

2   Add the ground cumin, ground coriander, chilli powder and paprika. Stir-fry for 1 minute to cook out the spices, then remove from the heat and set aside.

3   Brown the beef mince for 2–3 minutes in a large dry frying pan over a high heat. Drain off excess oil from the pan and add the tomato purée and Worcestershire sauce. Stir-fry over a low heat for 3–4 minutes. Remove from the heat.

4   Add the beef mince mixture to the stockpot with the vegetables. Then add the tinned tomatoes, beef stock, dried oregano, cinnamon stick and black pepper. Mix well, place over a high heat and bring to the boil.

5   When the mixture reaches boiling point, place a tight-fitting lid on top, reduce the heat to the lowest available setting and simmer for 10 minutes. Then, remove the cinnamon stick and continue to simmer for a further 35 minutes.

6   Add the kidney beans and chocolate. Mix well. Simmer for a further 15–20 minutes, adding a little water if the pan is starting to look dry.

7   Serve with boiled rice, fried potatoes and soured cream, or as a topping for a baked potato. Divide any leftover chilli into portion sizes and freeze for future use. The chilli will freeze well for up to 3 months.

Chilli Non Carne Vegetable Chilli (American Fast-food Style)

SERVES 3–4

2 tablespoons olive oil
½ red pepper, finely chopped
½ green pepper, finely chopped
½ yellow pepper, finely chopped
5 green finger chilli peppers, finely chopped
2 small onions, finely chopped
1 apple, peeled, cored and finely chopped
4 garlic cloves, crushed
1 x 400g/14oz tin peeled plum tomatoes
1 tablespoon chilli powder
1 tablespoon dried Italian herbs
1 teaspoon dried mixed herbs
1 teaspoon cayenne pepper
½ teaspoon ground turmeric
1 x 400g/14 oz tin kidney beans, rinsed and drained
Grated Cheddar cheese and raw onion slices, to serve
Sea salt and freshly ground black pepper

1   Heat the oil in a large stockpot over a medium heat. Add the red
    pepper, green pepper, yellow pepper, chilli peppers, onions and
    apple. Stir fry for 5–6 minutes, then add the garlic and fry for 1
    minute more.
2   Add the tinned tomatoes and 1.2 litres/2 pints of water. Add the
    chilli powder, Italian herbs, mixed herbs, cayenne pepper and
    turmeric, and season with a pinch each of sea salt and black pepper.
    Stir to combine.
3   Bring the contents of the pan to the boil, reduce the heat to low and
    place a lid on the pan. Simmer for 1½ hours or until the liquid is
    reduced and the sauce has thickened.

4   Mash the vegetables in the pan until the mixture has a mince-like consistency. Add the drained kidney beans and simmer on a low heat for a further 10 minutes.

5   Serve the vegetable chilli topped with grated Cheddar cheese and raw onion slices. Leftover chilli will store well in the freezer for up to 3 months.

Mac 'n' Cheese (American Fast-food Style)

The ultimate comfort food, this delicious macaroni cheese uses both creamy mozzarella and sharp Cheddar to create a dish bursting with flavour. Of course, leftovers *must* be turned into Mac 'n' Cheese Bites (see p.20).

SERVES 1–2
120g/4oz of macaroni pasta (dry weight)
1 tablespoon butter
1 tablespoon plain flour
200ml/7fl oz semi-skimmed milk
Pinch of ground nutmeg
75g/3oz mild or medium Cheddar cheese, grated, plus extra for topping (optional)
30g/1oz mozzarella cheese, grated, plus extra for topping (optional)
1 tablespoon mayonnaise
Thinly sliced salad tomatoes for topping (optional)
Sea salt and freshly ground black pepper

1   Put 2 litres/3½ pints of water into a large pan, salt the water with a large pinch of sea salt and then bring to the boil.
2   Add the macaroni and return to the boil. Simmer the pasta for 7–8 minutes, stirring only to prevent sticking, until it is just cooked.
3   Meanwhile, melt the butter over a low heat in a small pan. Add the flour and mix well to form a roux or thick paste. Add the milk a little at a time, whisking continuously between each addition, until you have added all the milk and have a smooth, lump-free sauce. Stir in the ground nutmeg, season with sea salt and pepper, then add the Cheddar and mozzarella cheeses and mayonnaise. Mix well and simmer until the cheeses melt and the sauce begins to thicken slightly.

4 Drain the cooked macaroni and return it to the pan. Pour in the cheese sauce and stir well to coat the macaroni in the sauce completely.

5 Serve immediately, or pour the coated macaroni into an ovenproof dish, top with sliced tomatoes and/or extra grated Cheddar and mozzarella and finish under a hot grill to create a crispy cheese topping. Serve with garlic bread.

Loaded Jalapeño Nachos (American Fast-food Style)

SERVES 1

1 tablespoon butter

1 tablespoon plain flour

120ml/4fl oz semi-skimmed milk, plus extra if needed

4 processed cheese slices

1 large handful tortilla chips

3 tablespoons salsa (see below)

2 tablespoons jarred jalapeño peppers, patted dry

Sea salt

FOR THE SALSA (SERVES 1–2):

1 large tomato, quartered, seeds removed, flesh chopped

½ red onion, finely chopped

½ red pepper, finely chopped

½ green pepper, finely chopped

1 finger of chilli pepper, finely sliced

1 garlic clove, crushed

¼ teaspoon dried parsley

¼ teaspoon salt

Pinch of black pepper

1 tablespoon olive oil

2 teaspoons lime juice

1   First make the salsa. Put the tomato in a large bowl with the onion, peppers, chilli and garlic. Mix thoroughly, then add the remaining ingredients, mix again and refrigerate for at least 1 hour before using.

2   When you're ready to eat, melt the butter in a small pan over a low heat, then add the plain flour and mix well.

3   Add the semi-skimmed milk and stir until the mixture is combined. Simmer for 1–2 minutes, stirring constantly, until you have a smooth sauce.

4   Add the processed cheese slices and mix well. Simmer for a further
    5 minutes, until the sauce becomes bright yellow and thickens. Add
    a little extra milk if the mixture becomes too thick; or simmer for
    longer if the mixture is too thin. Season with a pinch of sea salt, mix
    well and set aside.

5   Arrange the tortilla chips on a large plate. Scatter the fresh salsa
    over the chips, then the jalapeños, then 3–4 tablespoons of the
    cheese sauce.

6   Microwave the loaded nachos for 30–40 seconds on full heat until
    piping hot. Remove the plate from the microwave, allow to cool for
    1 minute and serve. If you like, you can add more toppings to the
    nachos: try refried beans, chilli con carne and soured cream.

Milkshakes (American Fast-food Style)

VANILLA SHAKE

SERVES 1
200ml/7fl oz vanilla ice cream
125ml/4fl oz semi-skimmed milk
4 teaspoons white sugar, plus extra to taste (optional)

1   Put the vanilla ice cream, semi-skimmed milk and sugar in a blender and blitz until fully combined.
2   Add more sugar to taste, if desired, and serve immediately.

CHOCOLATE SHAKE

As the Vanilla Shake, but replace the 4 teaspoons of white sugar with 1 tablespoon of chocolate-flavour milkshake powder.

STRAWBERRY SHAKE

As the Vanilla Shake, but replace the 4 teaspoons of white sugar with 1½ tablespoons of strawberry-flavour milkshake powder.

PART 2

Kebab Shop

Kebabs of one kind or another are eaten all around the world. The word 'kebab' is Turkish in origin and it's often suggested that this style of food was invented by medieval fighters who used their swords as skewers, holding pieces of meat over an open flame. In truth, kebabs reflect cooking in its simplest terms. Even as modern technology introduces various new kitchen tools and gadgets, you can't beat the simplicity and depth of flavour offered as a result of cooking marinated meats over an open flame. In any country, good weather offers the chance to eat outdoors and kebabs are the number-one barbecue choice.

For most home cooks, the chance to cook outdoors over an open flame comes around all too infrequently. For that reason, we need to find alternative cooking methods that best recreate the same flavours and aromas associated with good kebabs. The cooking methods used in this chapter will offer excellent results; however, do experiment with your barbecue or charcoal grill should the weather be kind enough to allow it.

The classic 'Lamb Doner' kebab is perhaps the most commonly eaten fast-food kebab in the western world. It has gained a somewhat unfortunate reputation over time, with many critics pointing to high levels of sea salt and fat within poor-quality takeaway offerings. Although not without some truth, these stories do not do justice to the high-quality kebabs that are available from some of the country's most talented takeaway restaurant chefs. In many parts of the world, good kebabs are eaten not only as a late-night snack, but also as a healthy, nutritious lunch or dinner. Using fresh meat and spices, marinated over time to intensify the flavours, the chef creates a meal that is both healthy and delicious.

By creating your own kebabs in the same way with the recipes contained in this chapter, you'll be sure of capturing that authentic kebab flavour in the healthiest way possible.

The recipes included here should of course be served with a selection of flatbreads, salads and sauces. Traditionally, kebabs are served with pitta bread. In recent times, an alternative choice known as a 'King Kebab' has been added to many takeaway menus. This dish resembles a traditional kebab in almost every way; however, it is often slightly larger in size and is accompanied by naan bread as opposed to pitta.

Quarter Pounder Burger (Kebab-shop Style)

SERVES 1

About 115g/4oz beef mince (minimum 20% fat)
1 large sesame-seed burger bun, halved
1 slice of processed cheese (optional)
¼ small onion, diced
1 tablespoon diced fresh tomato
1 small handful of shredded iceberg lettuce
1 small handful of shredded white or red cabbage
1 tablespoon of Chilli Kebab Sauce (see p.98)
Sea salt and freshly ground black pepper

1 Roll the beef mince into a ball. Place it on a sheet of greaseproof paper, and position another sheet on top. Flatten the ball into a thin circular patty, slightly bigger than the size of your burger bun. Cover and place in the coldest part of the fridge for 1–2 hours.

2 Preheat the oven to its lowest setting.

3 Heat a griddle pan on a high heat. Toast the burger-bun halves cut-sides down in the pan for around 30 seconds, or until golden and toasted. Set aside.

4 Place the burger patty onto the hot dry griddle pan, reduce the heat to medium and cook, untouched, for 2–3 minutes. Flip the burger, season with a generous pinch each of sea salt and black pepper and cook for a further 2 minutes or until cooked through and the juices run clear. Add the cheese slice, if using, 30 seconds before the burger is cooked. Set aside to keep warm.

5 Combine the onion, tomato, shredded lettuce and cabbage with the chilli kebab sauce and mix well. Slide the burger onto the bun bottom and top with 1–2 tablespoons of the salad and sauce. Wrap the burger loosely in foil or baking paper and place in the oven for 2–3 minutes to heat through and allow the flavours to combine. Serve with French fries.

Tex-Mex Burger
(Kebab-shop Style)

SERVES 1

About 115g/4oz beef mince (minimum 20% fat)

¼ teaspoon Cajun spice mix (see opposite)

½ teaspoon Worcestershire sauce

2 tablespoons finely chopped onion

1 small garlic clove, crushed

1 large sesame seed burger bun, halved

1 tablespoon mayonnaise, mixed with a small pinch of Cajun spice mix

1 small handful shredded iceberg lettuce

1 slice of processed cheese

1 tablespoon jarred jalapeño peppers, patted dry with kitchen paper and chopped

Sea salt and freshly ground black pepper

1 In a small bowl, combine the mince, Cajun spice mix, Worcestershire sauce, onion and garlic, and season with a pinch each of sea salt and pepper. Mix well until thoroughly combined.

2 Roll the beef mince into a ball. Place it on a sheet of greaseproof paper, and position another sheet on top. Flatten the ball into a thin circular patty, slightly bigger than the size of your burger bun. Cover and place in the coldest part of the fridge for 1–2 hours. (You can freeze it at this point, if you like.)

3 Preheat the oven to its lowest setting.

4 Heat a griddle pan on a high heat. Toast the burger-bun halves cut-sides down in the pan for around 30 seconds, or until golden and toasted. Set aside.

5 Place the burger patty onto the hot dry griddle pan and cook for 2–3 minutes; apply very gentle pressure with a spatula to ensure even browning. Flip the burger. Season with a little sea salt and pepper

and cook for a further 2 minutes or until cooked through and the juices run clear.

6   Spread the mayonnaise on the bun lid and add the shredded lettuce. Place the processed cheese slice on the bun bottom. Place the burger patty on top of the cheese-topped bun and add the chopped jalapeño peppers.

7   Place the bun lid on the dressed bun bottom. Wrap the burger loosely in foil or baking paper and place in the oven for 3–4 minutes to heat through and allow the flavours to combine. Serve with French fries.

Cajun Spice Mix (Mexican Style)

This mixture is so easy to prepare and far less expensive than shop bought varieties.

MAKES 1 SMALL TUB
1½ teaspoons salt
½ teaspoon black pepper
1 teaspoon dried oregano
¼ teaspoon dried thyme
1 teaspoon paprika
1 teaspoon cayenne pepper
¼ teaspoon garlic powder
¼ teaspoon onion granules
¼ teaspoon cumin powder
Pinch of sugar

1   In a large bowl, combine the salt, black pepper, dried oregano, dried thyme, paprika, cayenne pepper, garlic powder, onion granules, cumin powder and sugar.

2   Mix thoroughly and store in a sealed container.

Lamb Burger (Kebab-shop Style)

SERVES 1

About 115g/4oz lamb mince (minimum 20% fat)
¼ small onion, finely chopped
¼ teaspoon ground cumin
Small handful of coriander leaves, finely chopped
1 large burger bun, halved
1 tablespoon tzatziki (see p.100) or raita
Sea salt and freshly ground black pepper

1   In a large bowl, combine the lamb mince, chopped onion, ground cumin and fresh coriander. Season with a pinch each of sea salt and pepper and mix thoroughly until all of the ingredients are distributed evenly throughout the meat.

2   Roll the lamb mince into a ball. Place it on a sheet of greaseproof paper, and position another sheet on top. Flatten the ball into a thin circular patty, slightly bigger than the size of your burger bun. Cover and place in the coldest part of the fridge for 1–2 hours.

3   Heat a griddle pan on a high heat. Toast the burger-bun halves cut-sides down in the pan for around 30 seconds, or until golden and toasted. Set aside.

4   Place the burger patty onto the hot dry griddle pan and cook for 2–3 minutes; apply very gentle pressure with a spatula to ensure even browning. Flip the burger. Season with a little sea salt and pepper and cook for a further 2 minutes or until cooked through and the juices run clear.

5   Place the cooked burger patty onto the bun lid and top with the tzatziki or raita.

6   Add the bun bottom, invert and serve immediately with Pitta Salad (see p.94) and French fries.

Chickpea Burger (Kebab-shop Style)

SERVES 2

1 x 400g/14oz tin chickpeas
1 garlic clove, crushed
½ teaspoon ground cumin
¼ teaspoon ground coriander
Pinch of cayenne pepper
⅓ teaspoon of sea salt
Pinch of black pepper
2–3 tablespoons gram (chickpea) flour, plus a little extra for
   dusting
Vegetable oil, for deep frying
2 large sesame seed buns, halved
2 tablespoons tomato ketchup
2 tablespoons mayonnaise
2 small handfuls shredded iceberg lettuce

1   In a large pot, combine the chickpeas, garlic, ground cumin, ground
    coriander, cayenne pepper, sea salt and black pepper. Crush the
    mixture thoroughly with a potato masher until it becomes smooth.
2   Add the gram flour and mix thoroughly once again. Dust your hands
    with more gram flour and form half of the mixture into a large ball.
    Compress the mixture into a large burger-shaped patty and arrange
    on a plate. Repeat the process with the remaining mixture to give
    you two patties. Cover and set aside in the fridge for at least 2 hours,
    or overnight if possible. This will help the burgers to stay together
    as they cook.
3   Preheat the oven to its lowest setting.
4   When you're ready to cook the burgers, set your deep fryer to
    180°C/350°F. Alternatively, fill a wok or large frying pan one third
    full with vegetable oil and heat to 180°C/350°F. The oil is ready
    when a few breadcrumbs dropped into the oil sizzle immediately.
    Keep the burger patties in the fridge until you are ready to cook,

then drop them in and deep-fry them for 3–4 minutes or until crisp and golden.

5   Meanwhile, place a dry frying pan onto a medium heat. Toast the burger bun halves cut-sides down in the pan for about 30 seconds or until golden and toasted.

6   Remove the chickpea burgers from the oil and drain off any excess on kitchen paper. Place one patty on to each bun bottom and dress with ketchup and mayonnaise. Top with shredded lettuce and finish off with the bun lids. Wrap the burgers in foil or baking paper, invert and place in the oven for 2–3 minutes to heat through and allow the flavours to combine. Serve with French fries.

Lamb Doner Kebab
(Kebab-shop Style)

Traditionally, the lamb doner kebab is cooked on a standing rotisserie and thinly sliced to order. This home version is roasted in the oven and uses a classic doner spice mix to capture that authentic takeaway flavour.

SERVES 3–4

1 teaspoon plain flour
½ teaspoon garlic powder
½ teaspoon onion powder or onion granules
¼ teaspoon cayenne pepper
Pinch of paprika
Pinch of ground coriander
1 teaspoon dried oregano
½ teaspoon dried Italian herbs
1 teaspoon sea salt
½ teaspoon black pepper
500g/1lb 2 oz lamb mince

1   Preheat the oven to 180°C/350°F/Gas Mark 4.
2   In a large bowl, combine the plain flour, garlic powder, onion powder, cayenne pepper, paprika, coriander, oregano, Italian herbs, sea salt and black pepper. Mix well.
3   Add the lamb mince and mix thoroughly for 2–3 minutes.
    Take out all of your aggression on the kebab mixture, punching and kneading until no air pockets remain and the kebab meat is extremely smooth. This step is vital in achieving thin slices of doner meat.
4   Shape the seasoned mince into a loaf and place it on a baking tray lined with greaseproof paper.
5   Bake in the middle shelf of the oven for 40 minutes, then remove the kebab from the oven and use tongs to carefully turn the

kebab loaf over. Return the kebab to the oven for a further 40 minutes, until it is cooked and browned on all sides.

6 Once cooked, remove the doner from the oven and cover tightly with foil. Allow it to rest for 10 minutes.

7 Slice the doner meat as thinly as possible and serve with Pitta Salad (see p.94), Chilli Kebab Sauce (p.98) and Garlic Kebab Sauce (p.99).

Lamb Shish Kebab
(Kebab-shop Style)

SERVES 1–2

50ml/2fl oz olive oil

1 tablespoon Worcestershire sauce

2 tablespoons lemon juice

¼ onion

2 cloves of garlic

1 teaspoon ground cumin

½ teaspoon smoked paprika

1 teaspoon dried oregano

½ teaspoon dried rosemary

¼ teaspoon black pepper

250g/½lb boneless lamb leg steak

1 In a blender, combine the olive oil, Worcestershire sauce, lemon juice, onion, garlic, ground cumin, smoked paprika, dried oregano, dried rosemary and black pepper.

2 Trim any excess fat from the lamb leg steak and cut the meat into several medium–large pieces. Put the lamb in a bowl or food-safe bag, along with the blended ingredients. Mix well, cover and set aside the fridge for at least 4 hours, or overnight if possible.

3 Preheat the oven to 200°C/400°F/Gas Mark 6.

4 Arrange the lamb pieces on a wire rack over a roasting tray and bake on the highest oven shelf for 10 minutes. Turn the lamb pieces and bake for a further 6 minutes, then turn again and bake for a further 3–4 minutes or until just beginning to char.

5 Remove the lamb and set aside on a plate or serving dish to rest for 2–3 minutes. Serve with Pitta Salad (see p.94) and kebab sauces.

Lamb Kofta Kebab (Kebab-shop Style)

SERVES 3–4

500g/1lb 2oz lamb mince
1 onion, grated or very finely chopped
1 clove of garlic, finely chopped
2 finger chilli peppers, very finely chopped
¼ teaspoon allspice
½ teaspoon sweet paprika
½ teaspoon ground cumin
½ teaspoon sea salt
¼ teaspoon black pepper
1 egg
Oil, for frying

1   In a bowl, combine the lamb mince, onion, garlic, chilli peppers, allspice, sweet paprika, cumin, sea salt and black pepper.
2   Crack the egg into the bowl and mix well. Punch the kebab mixture well and mix thoroughly for 2–3 minutes, until extremely smooth, then divide the kofta mixture into 10–12 pieces.
3   Using wet hands shape each piece into a sausage shape and press down gently in the middle of each kofta. Heat a little oil in a griddle or frying pan over a medium–high heat. When the pan is hot, add the kofta pieces and cook for around 8–10 minutes, turning occasionally, until cooked through and golden on all sides. Serve with Pitta Salad (see p.94) and kebab sauces or (see p.98 and 99).

Lamb Seekh Kebab (Kebab-shop Style)

SERVES 1–2

½ small onion
½ green finger chilli pepper
1 teaspoon Garlic & Ginger Paste (see p.217)
½ teaspoon ground cumin
½ teaspoon ground coriander
½ teaspoon paprika
Pinch of cayenne pepper
¼ teaspoon sea salt
1 small handful of coriander
1 small handful of mint
250g/½lb lamb mince

1   Preheat the oven to 200°C/400°F/Gas Mark 6 and the grill to high.
2   Put the onion, chilli pepper, garlic & ginger paste, cumin, coriander, paprika, cayenne pepper, sea salt, coriander and mint in a blender and blitz for 1–2 minutes, scraping the side of the blender occasionally until the ingredients are fully combined. Alternatively, you can place the ingredients in a pestle and mortar and pound to a paste.
3   Transfer the blended mixture to a large bowl. Add the lamb mince and mix thoroughly until fully combined.
4   Using wet hands, divide the mixture into 3–4 sausage shapes. You can shape the kebabs around skewers, if you like.
5   Arrange the kebabs on a wire rack over a roasting tray and bake in the oven for about 6 minutes, then turn them over and bake for a further 6 minutes until they are cooked through and evenly browned on all sides.
6   Finish the kebabs under the hot grill (or on a hot griddle pan), cooking for a further 3–4 minutes until charred all over. Serve with Pitta Salad (see p.94) and kebab sauces (see p.98 and 99).

Shami Kebab (Indian-restaurant Style)

SERVES 3–4

1 onion, finely chopped
1 teaspoon garlic powder
½ teaspoon ground ginger
1½ teaspoons ground cumin
Pinch of ground coriander
½ teaspoon turmeric
½ teaspoon chilli powder
Pinch of paprika
1 heaped teaspoon dried fenugreek leaves
115g/4oz gram (chickpea) flour
500g/1lb 2oz lamb mince

1 Preheat the grill to medium–high.
2 In a large bowl, combine the chopped onion, garlic powder, ginger, cumin, coriander, turmeric, chilli powder, paprika, dried fenugreek leaves and gram flour. Mix well, then add the lamb mince and mix again thoroughly.
3 Using slightly wet hands, knead the seasoned mince mixture with your fist and work it together for 2–3 minutes until the texture is completely smooth and the spices and gram flour are evenly mixed.
4 Divide the mince mixture into 8 balls and press each one down gently to form small burger-shaped patties.
5 Arrange the kebabs on a grill tray and place them under the grill for 6–8 minutes or until cooked through, turning occasionally. Serve the kebabs with Chapatis (see p.205) and Onion Salad (see p.96).

Sarbeni Kebab (Kebab-shop Style)

This famous dish is based on 'lahmacun', also known as Turkish pizza. Many kebab shops now offer this spicy meat topped bread as an alternative to pitta and naan bread, topped and often rolled or wrapped with generous portions of kebab meat, salad and sauce. For a pizza-style twist, try topping the sarbeni bread with mozzarella cheese a minute or two before it leaves the oven.

SERVES 1

100g/3½oz plain flour, plus extra for dusting
50g/2oz wholemeal bread flour
¼ teaspoon sugar
¼ teaspoon fast-action dried yeast
¼ teaspoon sea salt
1 tablespoon olive oil, plus extra for coating
About 55g/2oz beef or lamb mince
2 tablespoons mix of red pepper, green pepper and white onion,
    finely chopped (approximately ½ pepper total)
1 garlic clove, crushed
Pinch of paprika
Pinch of dried parsley
Chicken, lamb or beef kebabs, cooked, to serve
Sea salt and freshly ground black pepper

1   In a large bowl, combine the plain flour, wholemeal bread
    flour, sugar, yeast, sea salt and olive oil. Mix well, and slowly add
    about 60ml/2fl oz water until the dough comes together.
2   Dust a work surface with flour and tip out the dough. Knead
    thoroughly for 3–4 minutes, until the dough becomes
    smooth.
3   Shape the dough into a ball, return to the bowl and toss in a drop of
    olive oil until coated. Brush a sheet of cling film with some olive oil,

wrap the dough in it and set aside for about 1 hour or until doubled in size.

4   Preheat the oven to 200°C/400°F/Gas Mark 6. Preheat a pizza stone in the oven, too, if you have one.

5   In a small bowl, combine the beef or lamb mince, pepper and onion mixture, garlic, paprika and dried parsley. Season with a pinch each of sea salt and black pepper and mix well.

6   Remove the dough from the cling film and use a rolling pin to roll it out on a floured surface to around 25cm/10 inches in diameter. Lightly oil a pizza tray with the remaining olive oil and place the dough on top, or use the preheated pizza stone.

7   Carefully press the prepared mince mixture onto the top of the dough until it is completely covered.

8   Place the tray or stone into the oven and cook the sarbeni bread for 8–10 minutes or until the dough becomes crispy around the edges and the meat is cooked through.

9   Remove the cooked sarbeni bread from the oven and immediately top with cooked chicken, lamb or beef kebabs. Serve with Chilli Kebab Sauce (see p.98), Garlic Kebab Sauce (p.99) and onion salad (p.96).

Chicken Doner Kebab (Kebab-shop Style)

This classic chicken doner soaks up a marinade based on the one used by many kebab wholesalers and sold in thousands of kebab shops around the UK.

SERVES 1–2

75ml/2½fl oz semi-skimmed milk

1 tablespoon olive oil

1 teaspoon paprika

2 garlic cloves, crushed

1 teaspoon tomato purée

2 teaspoons soy sauce

¼ teaspoon hot Madras curry powder

1 teaspoon dried thyme

½ teaspoon dried oregano

1 teaspoon natural red food colouring (optional)

4 medium skinless, boneless chicken thighs (about 226g/8oz total weight)

1 teaspoon vegetable oil

Sea salt and freshly ground black pepper

1   First, make a marinade. In a large bowl or food-safe bag, add the semi-skimmed milk, olive oil, paprika, garlic, tomato purée, soy sauce, hot Madras curry powder, dried thyme and dried oregano. Season with a pinch each of sea salt and pepper and add the natural red food colour, if using. Mix well.

2   Trim any excess fat from the chicken thighs and cut each thigh into 2 large pieces. Add the chicken pieces to the marinade and mix well. Cover the bowl and leave the chicken to marinate for at least 4 hours, or overnight if possible, in the fridge.

3   Heat the vegetable oil in a dry frying pan on a medium heat. Remove the chicken from the marinade and carefully drop the

pieces into the pan. Cook for 10 –12 minutes, turning once, until the chicken is golden all over and just cooked through. Remove the chicken from the pan and slice into thin strips.

4   Place the frying pan on a high heat. Return the chicken slices to the pan and stir-fry for a further 30 seconds until piping hot and just charred. Remove the chicken from the pan and serve with pitta or Chapatis (see p.205), Onion Salad (p.205) and kebab sauces (see p.98 and 99).

Chicken BBQ Kebab (Kebab-shop Style)

SERVES 1

2 tablespoons olive oil

2 tablespoons lemon juice

1 tablespoon Worcestershire sauce

½ teaspoon garlic powder

½ teaspoon onion powder

¼ teaspoon paprika

¼ teaspoon sea salt

¼ teaspoon black pepper

1 large skinless, boneless chicken breast fillet (about 115g/4oz weight)

1　First, make a marinade. In a large bowl or food-safe bag, combine the olive oil, lemon juice, Worcestershire sauce, garlic powder, onion powder, paprika, sea salt and black pepper. Mix well.

2　Trim any excess fat from the chicken breast and cut into 5–6 pieces. Add the chicken pieces to the marinade and mix well. Cover the bowl and leave the chicken to marinate for at least 4 hours, or overnight if possible, in the fridge.

3　Heat a dry griddle pan to a medium–high heat. Place the chicken pieces onto the griddle and leave to cook for 2–3 minutes, then turn the chicken pieces and continue cooking for a further 2–3 minutes, until cooked through and golden and charred on both sides. Serve with Pitta Salad (see p.94), Chilli Kebab Sauce (p.98) and Garlic Kebab Sauce (p.99).

Chicken Shashlik Kebab (Kebab-shop Style)

SERVES 1–2

2 tablespoons vegetable oil, plus extra for frying

2 tablespoons lemon juice

¼ teaspoon paprika

¼ teaspoon ground ginger

¼ teaspoon garlic powder

½ teaspoon ground cumin

¼ teaspoon garam masala

¼ teaspoon sugar

Small handful of coriander, finely chopped

1 large skinless, boneless chicken breast fillet (about 115g/4oz weight)

1 onion, chopped into large pieces

1 green pepper, chopped into large pieces

Sea salt and freshly ground black pepper

1   First, make a marinade. In a large bowl or food-safe bag, add the vegetable oil, lemon juice, paprika, ground ginger, garlic powder, cumin, garam masala, sugar and coriander, and season with a pinch each of sea salt and pepper.

2   Trim any excess fat from the chicken breast and cut into small thin pieces. Add the chicken pieces to the marinade and mix well. Cover the bowl and leave the chicken to marinate for at least 4 hours, or overnight if possible, in the fridge.

3   Preheat the oven to 200°C/400°F/Gas Mark 6.

4   Remove the chicken from the marinade. Arrange the chicken pieces on a wire rack over a roasting tray and bake for 8 minutes, then the chicken pieces and return to the oven for a further 8 minutes. Turn the chicken pieces once more and bake for a further 2–3 minutes, until just beginning to char.

5   When the chicken pieces are almost cooked, heat a little vegetable

oil in a frying pan over a medium heat. Add the chopped onion and green pepper and stir-fry for 5–6 minutes to soften. Set aside.

6   Arrange the chicken on a plate or serving tray and add the cooked onion and green pepper. Serve with Pitta Salad (p.94) and kebab sauces (see p.98 and 99).

Chicken Shawarma
(Kebab-shop Style)

SERVES 1

4 teaspoons tomato ketchup
1 tablespoon olive oil, plus extra for frying
3 tablespoons lemon juice
1 teaspoon white vinegar
½ teaspoon garlic powder
½ teaspoon paprika
¼ teaspoon allspice
Pinch of ground ginger
¼ teaspoon dried oregano
Pinch of dried thyme
½ teaspoon sea salt
2 skinless, boneless chicken thighs (about 225g/8oz total weight)
3–4 tablespoons light chicken stock or water
Chopped parsley, sliced tomatoes and thinly sliced onion, to serve

1   First, make a marinade. In a large bowl or food-safe bag,
    combine the tomato ketchup, olive oil, lemon juice, vinegar, garlic
    powder, paprika, allspice, ground ginger, oregano, thyme and sea
    salt. Mix well.
2   Trim any excess fat from the chicken thighs. Add the chicken
    thighs to the marinade, mix well and set aside for 30 minutes.
3   Heat a little olive oil in a frying pan on a high heat. Remove
    the chicken thighs from the marinade and carefully place them into
    the pan, reduce the heat to medium and leave to cook for 2 minutes,
    then turn the thighs over and cook for a further 2 minutes on the
    other side. Add the stock or water, reduce the heat to low and cook,
    covered, for a further 3–4 minutes.
4   Remove the chicken thighs from the pan, but leave the pan on the
    heat, and cut the thighs into small bite-sized pieces. Allow any
    remaining liquid to reduce in the pan as you cut the chicken.

5   Return the chicken pieces to the pan, increase the heat to medium and stir-fry for 1–2 minutes, until the chicken begins to char and sizzle in the pan.
6   Serve the chicken shawarma with a generous topping of parsley, sliced tomatoes and onions, and Pitta Breads (see p.91) and Garlic Kebab Sauce (see p.99).

Spicy Chicken Wings

SERVES 1–2

1 teaspoon cayenne pepper

¼ teaspoon chilli powder

1 tablespoon smoked paprika

2 teaspoons garlic powder

2 teaspoons onion powder

1 teaspoon dried oregano

1 teaspoon dried thyme

¼ teaspoon sea salt

¼ teaspoon black pepper

4 tablespoons vegetable oil

1 tablespoon lemon juice

6 chicken wings, split into 12 wing pieces, tips discarded

Lemon slices, to decorate

1   First, make a marinade. In a large bowl, combine the cayenne
    pepper, chilli powder, smoked paprika, garlic powder, onion powder,
    dried oregano, dried thyme, sea salt and black pepper.

2   Add the vegetable oil, lemon juice and chicken wing pieces. Rub the
    marinade thoroughly into each chicken wing piece. Cover the bowl
    and refrigerate for at least 4 hours, or overnight if possible.

3   Preheat the oven to 200°C/400°F/Gas Mark 6.

4   Remove the chicken wings from the marinade and arrange on
    a baking tray. Bake in the middle of the oven for 15 minutes. Turn
    the chicken pieces and cook for a further 15 minutes, then turn
    them again, move them to the top of the oven and cook for 5–6
    minutes more.

5   Turn the chicken pieces for a final time and return to the top
    of the oven for a final 5–6 minutes. Remove the chicken wings from
    the oven and arrange on a plate or serving dish. Serve decorated
    with lemon slices.

Pitta Breads (Kebab-shop Style)

MAKES 8 PITTA BREADS

400g/14oz strong white bread flour, plus extra for dusting
1 teaspoon sugar
1 x 7g sachet fast-action dried yeast
1 tablespoon black onion (nigella or kalonji) seeds (optional)
1 tablespoon olive oil
300ml/10½fl oz warm water
1 teaspoon sea salt

1   In a large bowl, combine the bread flour, sugar and yeast. Add
    the black onion seeds, if using, and stir again.
2   Add the olive oil and mix well, then add half the warm water and
    mix again to form a crumbly dough. Add the sea salt.
3   Slowly add the remaining water, working the dough with your
    hands, until it comes together.
4   Dust a work surface or board with flour and knead the dough
    for 3–4 minutes until smooth and elastic. Return the dough to the
    bowl and cover with a damp cloth. Set aside to rise for 1 hour.
5   Remove the dough from the bowl and knead again, to knock the air
    out of it. Divide the dough into 8 equal pieces and knead each one
    for a further 1 minute, then shape it into a ball. Place the pitta
    breads onto a baking tray, press down to flatten slightly, cover, and
    set aside to prove for 20 minutes.
6   Meanwhile, preheat the oven to 240°C/475°F/Gas Mark 9.
7   Place the baking tray in the oven and bake the pitta breads for 7–8
    minutes, until puffed up and golden. Remove from the oven and
    wrap with a clean damp dishcloth. This will help the pitta breads to
    soften a little. Serve the pitta breads with your favourite kebabs or
    simply toasted and sliced ready to dunk in hummus.

Kebab-shop Pizza
(Kebab-shop Style)

This recipe makes use of inexpensive supermarket-bought naan breads to create a pizza that very closely replicates those found in kebab shops. Of course, you can add any number of toppings – such as pepperoni, mushrooms, sweetcorn and so on – but remember that with pizza toppings, less is more. Go easy to ensure the pizza doesn't become overloaded.

SERVES 1

1 supermarket naan bread
1 tablespoon sweet Pizza Sauce (see p.225)
75g/3oz mozzarella cheese, grated
1 small salad tomato, halved and thinly sliced
Pinch of dried oregano, to decorate
Pinch of black pepper, to decorate

1 Heat the oven to 220°C/425°F/Gas Mark 7.
2 Place the naan bread on a baking tray. Spread the pizza sauce over the naan bread and add around one third of the mozzarella cheese. Top with sliced tomatoes and then add the remaining cheese.
3 Place the pizza in the oven and cook for around 10–12 minutes or until the cheese is melted and golden. Remove the pizza from the oven and sprinkle over the dried oregano and black pepper, to decorate. Serve the pizza in slices with Chilli Kebab Sauce (see p.98).

Doner Calzone (Kebab-shop Style)

SERVES 1

1 prepared 25cm/10-inch pizza base (see p.223)

2–3 tablespoons Pizza Sauce (see p.224)

100g/3½oz mozzarella cheese, grated, plus an extra handful for topping

10–12 thin slices of cooked Lamb Doner (see p.75)

2 tablespoons Spiced Onions (see p.180)

Pinch of dried oregano

Pinch of black pepper

1 Heat the oven to 220°C/425°F/Gas Mark 7.

2 Spread the pizza sauce thickly onto one half of the pizza base. Add the mozzarella cheese, lamb doner slices and spiced onions.

3 Fold the dough over the filling and press down at the edges to form a seal. Place on a baking tray or pizza stone and cook in the oven for 5 minutes.

4 Remove the tray from the oven and top the calzone with the extra mozzarella cheese. Return to the oven for a further 8–10 minutes, until the crust is golden and the cheese has melted.

5 Remove the calzone from the oven and sprinkle with dried oregano and black pepper. Serve with Chilli Kebab Sauce (p.98) and Onion Salad (see p.96).

Pitta Salad (Kebab-shop Style)

SERVES 2

2 red onions, finely sliced
1 carrot, peeled and grated
¼ cucumber, thinly sliced
3–4 red cabbage leaves, finely sliced
1 large handful shredded iceberg lettuce
1 salad tomato, halved and thinly sliced
Juice of half a lemon
2–3 tablespoons Chilli Kebab Sauce (see p.98)
1–2 Pickled Chilli Peppers (see p.95), to decorate
3 Pitta Breads (see p.91)

1   Preheat the grill to hot.
2   Place the sliced onions in a bowl of cold water for about 10 minutes.
    Drain in a sieve and pat dry with kitchen paper.
3   In a large bowl, combine the sliced onion, grated carrot, sliced
    cucumber, sliced cabbage leaves, shredded iceberg lettuce and
    sliced tomato. Add the lemon juice and stir to mix gently. Dress
    with the Chilli Kebab Sauce and decorate with the Pickled Chilli
    Peppers.
4   Grill the pitta breads under the hot grill for about 30 seconds on
    each side or until lightly warmed and toasted. Alternatively, use
    metal tongs to hold the pitta breads over an open flame on the hob
    and toast for about 30–40 seconds on each side or until the breads
    become slightly charred and crispy. Immediately wrap the flame-
    toasted pitta breads in foil and set aside for 1–2 minutes to soften.
5   Serve the pitta salad with your favourite kebabs.

Pickled Chilli Peppers (Kebab-shop Style)

These pickled chilli peppers are a great money saver and make a delicious topping to salads or kebabs.

MAKES ENOUGH TO FILL 1 X 200ML/7FL OZ JAR
75g/2½oz green and red finger chilli peppers
120ml/4fl oz white wine vinegar
1 garlic clove
½ bay leaf
Small pinch dried rosemary
1 teaspoon caster sugar

1   Cut the stems from the chilli peppers at the tip, leaving the chilli peppers sealed and unopened. Place the chilli peppers in a small pan, then add the white wine vinegar, garlic, bay leaf, dried rosemary and caster sugar.
2   Stir the mixture once, then place over a medium–high heat and bring to the boil. Reduce the heat and simmer for about 8 minutes to soften the chillies.
3   Transfer the pickled chilli peppers to a sterilised jam jar, and pour the cooking vinegar over the top, adding up to 75ml/2½fl oz more as necessary to completely cover the chillies.
4   Set the jar aside so that the contents cool completely, then secure the lid, and use as necessary. The chillies will keep for up to 1 month in the airtight jar.

Onion Salad (Kebab-shop Style)

This classic onion salad is served with almost every dish at kebab shops up and down the country.

SERVES 1–2
2 onions, finely sliced
¼ cucumber
1 large tomato
1 teaspoon mint sauce
Sea salt

1   Place the onion slices in a bowl of cold water for around 30 minutes. Drain well in a sieve and pat dry with kitchen paper.
2   Place the dried onion slices in a large bowl. Slice the cucumber in half and use a teaspoon to scrape out and discard the seeds. Finely chop the cucumber flesh and combine with the onions.
3   Quarter the tomato and use a knife to carefully remove the seeds. Finely chop the tomato flesh and combine with the onion and cucumber.
4   Add the mint sauce, mix thoroughly and set aside in the fridge for at least 1 hour before using. Season with a pinch of sea salt just before serving. Serve with Chicken Puri (see p.201) or with any Indian curry, kebab or pakora.

Variation
CABBAGE & ONION SALAD
Shred 4 white or red cabbage leaves and place them in a bowl with 50ml/2fl oz white vinegar and ½ teaspoon of sea salt. Soak for at least 1 hour. Rinse the cabbage with water and pat dry. Coat with 1 teaspoon of olive oil and add to the prepared onion salad.

Greek Salad (Kebab-shop Style)

SERVES 2

½ small red onion, finely chopped
½ cucumber, peeled and deseeded
3 plum tomatoes, deseeded and chopped
10–12 pitted black olives, sliced
Small handful of chopped lettuce
1 tablespoon lemon juice
3 tablespoons extra-virgin olive oil
½ teaspoon red wine vinegar
1 garlic clove, finely chopped
¼ teaspoon dried oregano
¼ teaspoon sea salt
¼ teaspoon black pepper
125g/4oz feta cheese, diced
Pitta Bread (see p.91), toasted, to serve

1   Place the chopped onion in a bowl of cold water for about 30 minutes. Drain well in a sieve and pat dry with kitchen paper.
2   In a large bowl, combine the red onion, cucumber, plum tomatoes, black olives and lettuce.
3   In a small bowl, make a dressing by combining the lemon juice, with the extra-virgin olive oil, red wine vinegar, chopped garlic, dried oregano, sea salt and black pepper.
4   Pour as much dressing over the prepared salad ingredients as you like, then toss the salad to coat in the dressing. Top with the feta cheese and serve with toasted pitta bread.

Chilli Kebab Sauce
(Kebab-shop Style)

The classic kebab-shop chilli sauce is packed full of vibrant,
zingy flavours. Perfect with any kebab, it also makes an
amazing dip for Kebab-shop Pizza.

MAKES 6–8 TUBS
200ml/7fl oz tomato ketchup
1 teaspoon mint sauce
1 salad tomato, quartered
1 small onion, quartered
1 red pepper, roughly chopped
½ teaspoon mild chilli powder
½ teaspoon sea salt
5 tablespoons mixed fruit cocktail (tinned or frozen)
75ml water

1   Put the tomato ketchup, mint sauce, salad tomato, onion, red
    pepper, chilli powder, sea salt and fruit cocktail in a blender with
    75ml/2½fl oz of water and blitz until smooth. Test the consistency
    of the sauce – it should pour easily – adding a further 1 tablespoon
    of water to loosen, if necessary. (The sauce may thicken over time:
    if that happens, simply thin it down with more water and mix well
    before serving.)
2   Pour the sauce into dip trays and set aside in the fridge for at least
    2 hours, or ideally overnight, before serving with your favourite
    kebabs or Kebab-shop Pizza (see p.92).

Garlic Kebab Sauce (Kebab-shop Style)

MAKES 1 TUB

3 tablespoons mayonnaise
1–2 tablespoons natural yogurt
1 teaspoon olive oil
¼–½ teaspoon garlic powder
Pinch of dried parsley or dried mixed herbs
1–2 tablespoons semi-skimmed milk, to thin the sauce if required
Sea salt

1 In a bowl or serving tub, combine the mayonnaise, natural yogurt, olive oil, garlic powder and dried parsley or mixed herbs. Season with a pinch of sea salt and mix thoroughly until well combined.
2 Add the milk to thin the sauce to the desired consistency, if necessary, then chill for 1–2 hours before serving.

Tzatziki (Kebab-shop Style)

SERVES 2

⅓ cucumber, peeled, deseeded and grated
1 tablespoon lemon juice
1 garlic clove, finely chopped
1 teaspoon olive oil
About 120ml/4fl oz natural yogurt
Pinch of paprika, to decorate
Sea salt

1 Squeeze the grated cucumber to remove some of the water and put the cucumber in a small bowl.
2 Add the lemon juice, chopped garlic, olive oil and natural yogurt, then season with a pinch of sea salt and mix well.
3 Refrigerate the tzatziki for at least 1 hour, before serving sprinkled with a little paprika. Serve with a Pitta Salad (see p.94)

PART 3

Chinese

The most important item of equipment required in Chinese cooking is undoubtedly the wok. A good-quality, well-seasoned wok will last a lifetime and is a worthy investment. Any large frying pan will provide an excellent substitute, providing it is large enough to enable quick stirring of the ingredients. Regardless of the type of pan, it's essential that you use a high heat when the final cooking process begins.

....

As with the Indian curry dishes, Chinese stir-fry cooking requires preparation in order to ensure that the final cooking of the meal happens quickly and easily. By preparing the ingredients in advance, your attention can remain focused on the wok and its ingredients, allowing you to ensure the pan is stirred constantly to prevent burning over a high heat.

People often comment on the silky and tender meat used in Chinese stir-fry dishes. This is achieved using a cornflour marinade similar to the one described in this chapter and takes no time at all to prepare. Unlike other marinades, which may need to be left overnight, this simple technique works in minutes. Almost all of the meats used in Chinese restaurant dishes begin life in this marinade, which protects the meat and seals the juices inside while cooking.

You can buy Chinese cooking ingredients from any good supermarket; however, it's well worth seeking out a large Chinese supermarket if there is one in your area, where you're sure to find a huge range of Chinese and other Far Eastern ingredients.

The recipes in this chapter are based around the dishes typically offered by Chinese takeaways and restaurants. Stir-fry cooking is an ideal way to combine various meats and vegetables, however, so do experiment with other ingredients. Chow mein and fried rice dishes are particularly versatile and work extremely well with any sliced vegetables.

Store-cupboard ingredients useful to have in stock in order to cook your favourite Chinese takeaway food include:

Light soy sauce
Dark soy sauce
Oyster sauce
Shaoxing rice wine
Rice wine vinegar
White vinegar
Potato flour or cornflour
Vegetable oil
Garlic
Ginger
Chinese five-spice
Toasted sesame oil
Tomato ketchup
White sugar
Brown sugar

Chicken Noodle Soup (Chinese-takeaway Style)

Fragrant and full of flavour, this soup is the perfect pick-me-up.

SERVES 2–3
1 nest of egg noodles
1 litre/1¾ pints Chinese Stock (see p.166) or chicken stock
1 garlic clove, crushed or finely chopped
1 x 2.5cm/1-inch piece of ginger, grated or finely chopped
2 skinless, boneless chicken thigh fillets
5–6 tablespoons sweetcorn (tinned or frozen)
1–2 spring onions, finely sliced
1 teaspoon light soy sauce, plus extra to serve
Dash of dark soy sauce
Coriander leaves, to decorate

1 Place the egg noodles in a large pot and cover with boiling water. Allow to stand for 2–3 minutes or until the noodles just begin to soften. Rinse the noodles with cold water, drain and set aside.

2 In a large pan, bring the Chinese or chicken stock to the boil, then reduce the heat to low and add the garlic and ginger, and the chicken thigh fillets. Cover the pan with a lid and simmer on a low heat for 7–8 minutes, until the chicken is cooked through.

3 Remove the chicken thighs from the pan and place on a chopping board. Shred the chicken into small pieces and return to the pot. Add the sweetcorn, spring onions, light soy sauce and dark soy sauce. Simmer for a further 3–4 minutes to heat through.

4 Ladle the soup into serving bowls, decorate with coriander leaves and serve with extra light soy sauce on the side.

Chicken & Sweetcorn Soup (Chinese-takeaway Style)

SERVES 1–2

1 egg white

350ml/12fl oz Chinese Stock (see p.166) or chicken stock

1 large handful cooked roast chicken, shredded

3–4 tablespoons tinned creamed sweetcorn

Dash of light soy sauce

2 teaspoons cornflour mixed with 2 tablespoons of water to
    make a paste

1 spring onion, finely sliced

Dash of toasted sesame oil

1   Whisk the egg white for a few seconds to make it pourable and set
    aside.

2   Pour the stock into a wok or saucepan. Place over a high heat and
    bring to the boil. Reduce the heat to low, and add the cooked
    chicken and tinned creamed sweetcorn. Mix well and simmer for
    2 minutes.

3   Add the soy sauce and mix well again, then add the cornflour paste
    and stir it through to thicken the soup slightly.

4   Simmer the soup for a further 2 minutes, then slowly drizzle in the
    whisked egg white, stirring continuously. Simmer for a further 30
    seconds. Pour the soup into a serving bowl and garnish with the
    spring onion. Add the toasted sesame oil and serve.

Crispy Chicken Wings in Salt & Chilli (Chinese-takeaway Style)

SERVES 2

1 egg, beaten

120g/4oz potato starch or cornflour, seasoned with a little sea salt

6 chicken wings, split into 12 wing pieces and tips discarded

Vegetable oil, for frying

½ onion, finely chopped

1–2 spring onions, finely chopped

½ green pepper, finely chopped

2 garlic cloves, crushed

1–2 red or green finger chilli peppers, finely sliced

½–1 teaspoon Sea Salt & Szechuan Seasoning (see p.163)

1–2 tablespoons Shaoxing rice wine

1 Put the beaten egg in one bowl and the seasoned potato starch or cornflour in another.

2 When you're ready to cook the wings, set your deep fryer to 180°C/350°F. Alternatively, fill a wok or large frying pan one third full with vegetable oil and heat to 180°C/350°F. The oil is ready when a few breadcrumbs dropped into the oil sizzle immediately. Keeping one hand dry, dip the chicken-wing pieces first into the egg and then into the seasoned flour. Carefully place each breaded wing into the hot oil and fry for around 8–10 minutes or until cooked through and crispy. Remove from the oil using a slotted spoon, drain on kitchen paper and set aside.

3 In a wok or large frying pan, heat a little oil over a low heat. Add the onion, spring onions, green pepper, garlic and chilli. Increase the heat to medium and stir-fry for 30 seconds, until fragrant and aromatic.

4 Add the cooked wings to the wok and season generously with
the Sea Salt & Szechuan Seasoning. Stir well and add the rice wine.
Stir a final time and tip out the chicken wings on to a serving dish.
Serve with Plain Chow Mein Noodles (see p.158) and Sweet Chilli
Sauce (p.165).

Baked Chicken Wings in Salt & Chilli (Chinese-takeaway Style)

SERVES 2

500g/1lb 2oz chicken wings, jointed, wing-tips removed
1 tablespoon vegetable oil
1 small onion, diced
½ green pepper, diced
1 green chilli pepper, finely sliced
1 red chilli pepper, finely sliced
4 garlic cloves, finely chopped or crushed
2 spring onions, finely sliced
1 generous teaspoon Sea Salt & Szechuan Seasoning (see p.163)
1 tablespoon Shaoxing rice wine
Dash of toasted sesame oil

1   Preheat the oven to 190°C/375°F/Gas Mark 5 and line a baking tray with foil.
2   Arrange the chicken wings on a wire rack above the lined baking tray and bake the chicken wings for about 35 minutes, until cooked through and crispy.
3   When the wings are almost ready, heat 1 tablespoon of vegetable oil in a wok or large frying pan over a medium heat. Add the diced onion and green pepper. Stir-fry for 2 minutes to soften then add the green chilli, red chilli, garlic and spring onion and stir-fry for 30 seconds more.
4   Add the cooked chicken wings to the wok, season generously with Sea Salt & Szechuan Seasoning and stir well for 30 seconds. Add the rice wine and stir well once more. Finish with toasted sesame oil and serve.

Chicken Wings in Hoisin Sauce (Chinese-takeaway Style)

SERVES 1–2

4 tablespoons tomato ketchup

4 tablespoons hoisin sauce

4 tablespoons honey

2 teaspoons light soy sauce

2 teaspoons dark soy sauce

2 teaspoons toasted sesame oil

1 teaspoon vegetable oil

6 chicken wings, split into 12 wing pieces, tips discarded

¼ teaspoon sea salt and ¼ teaspoon freshly ground black pepper

1 Preheat the oven to 180°C/350°F/Gas Mark 4.

2 In a large bowl, combine the tomato ketchup, hoisin sauce, honey, soy sauces and toasted sesame oil. Mix well and set aside.

3 In a separate bowl, combine the vegetable oil, sea salt, black pepper and chicken-wing pieces. Mix well by hand and arrange the wings on a baking tray. Cover loosely with foil.

4 Bake the wings for 30–40 minutes or until just cooked through. Remove from the oven and set aside to cool slightly.

5 Heat a dry griddle pan on a low–medium heat. Add the chicken wings to the pan and cook for 7–8 minutes, turning often and basting occasionally with the prepared sauce. Allow the sauce to caramelise.

6 When the wings are nicely charred, remove them from the pan and arrange them on a large plate. Serve as a starter to any Chinese meal, or simply as a snack.

Spare Ribs (Chinese-takeaway Style)

These classic Chinese ribs are flavoured with five-spice powder and can be served dry or with Chinese brown gravy (page 119).

SERVES 1–2
2 teaspoons Garlic & Ginger paste (see p.217)
8 tablespoons tomato ketchup
3 tablespoons honey
½ tablespoon Chinese five-spice
1 kg/2½lb pork ribs

1   First, make a marinade. In a bowl, combine the garlic and ginger paste, tomato ketchup, honey and Chinese five-spice. Mix well.

2   Add the pork ribs to the marinade and mix well until all of the ribs are coated. Cover the bowl and refrigerate for at least 4 hours, or overnight if possible.

3   Preheat the oven to 200°C/400°F/Gas Mark 6. Remove the pork ribs from the marinade and arrange on a rack over a roasting tray filled with a little water.

4   Place the ribs on the middle oven shelf and bake for 8 minutes. Turn the ribs and cook for a further 8 minutes. Turn the ribs once more, move to the top of the oven and cook for a further 8 minutes. Turn the ribs for a final time and return to the top of the oven for a final 8 minutes or until the ribs are cooked through and charred.

5   Remove the ribs from the oven and arrange on a plate or serving dish. Serve as a starter or side dish with any Chinese meal.

Sweet & Sour Ribs (Chinese-takeaway Style)

SERVES 1

¼ red pepper, chopped

¼ green pepper, chopped

¼ yellow pepper, chopped

½ onion, chopped

1 tinned pineapple ring, chopped

75ml/2½fl oz rice wine vinegar

2 tablespoons tomato ketchup

1 tablespoon white sugar

1 tablespoon brown sugar

½ teaspoon soy sauce

1 large pork loin steak (about 115g/4oz weight)

1 egg

6 tablespoons cornflour, plus a further 1 teaspoon mixed with
    2 tablespoons of water to make a paste

Vegetable oil, for deep frying, plus extra for stir frying

Sea salt and freshly ground black pepper

1   In a bowl, combine the red pepper, green pepper, yellow pepper,
    onion and pineapple. Set aside.

2   Make a sweet-and-sour sauce. Put the rice wine vinegar, 75ml of
    water, tomato ketchup, white sugar, brown sugar and soy sauce in a
    small pan over a high heat. Bring to the boil, reduce the heat to low
    and simmer for 2 minutes or until the sugar is dissolved. Set aside.

3   Trim any excess fat from the pork loin steak and cut into small bite-
    sized pieces, then season well with sea salt and pepper.

4   Whisk the egg a little in a large bowl and add the seasoned pork
    pieces. Mix thoroughly to coat the meat.

5   Put the cornflour in a separate bowl. Lift the pork pieces out
    of the egg mixture using a slotted spoon, discarding any excess egg.
    Place the pork in the bowl with the cornflour and toss well until

each piece is fully coated. Place the coated pork pieces onto a baking tray in a single layer in order to ensure they don't stick together.

6 When you're ready to cook the ribs, set your deep fryer to 180°C/350°F. Alternatively, fill a wok or large frying pan one third full with vegetable oil and heat to 180°C/350°F. The oil is ready when a few breadcrumbs dropped into the oil sizzle immediately. Carefully drop the pork pieces into the oil and fry for 3–4 minutes until crispy and just cooked through. Remove the pork from the pan, drain off any excess oil on kitchen paper and set aside.

7 Heat a wok or frying pan on a high heat. Add a little vegetable oil. Tip the prepared vegetables into the pan and stir-fry for 2–3 minutes. Reduce the heat to low and add the sweet-and-sour sauce. Cook for 20 seconds, then stir the cornflour paste and add slowly to the pan, stirring until the sauce thickens slightly. Add the cooked pork pieces and mix thoroughly. Serve with Egg Fried Rice (see p.157) or plain chow mein.

Spring Rolls (Chinese-takeaway Style)

SERVES 4

1 teaspoon vegetable oil

8-10 button mushrooms, finely sliced

1 onion, finely sliced

1 tablespoon rice wine

2 teaspoons light soy sauce

1½ teaspoons chinese 5-spice

½ teaspoon sea salt

¼ teaspoon black pepper

¼ teaspoon white pepper

Pinch of msg (optional)

200g beansprouts

Cooked meat (optional)

Frozen spring roll wrappers (16 mini or 8 large), defrosted as per pack instructions

1 tablespoon potato or cornflour, mixed with 1 tablespoon water

Oil for deep frying

1   Heat the oil in a wok over a high heat. Add the sliced mushrooms and onion. Stir-fry for 2–3 minutes. Add the rice wine, light soy sauce, 5-spice, sea salt, black pepper and white pepper. Add the msg if desired. Add the beansprouts along with 1–2 tablespoons of water. Stir-fry for a further 2–3 minutes. Pour the cooked ingredients into a sieve to drain any excess liquid and set aside to cool. After the filling has cooled, add cooked meat if desired.

2   When the filling has completely cooled, begin to assemble the spring rolls. Place some filling towards one corner of a spring roll wrapper. Roll the wrapper over the filling and roll upwards until the filling is encased. Fold in the sides and continue to roll. Add a little of the flour and water mix to the top of the spring roll wrapper as a glue and complete the roll to seal. Repeat the

process until all of the spring rolls are prepared. As each spring roll is prepared, place on a plate and keep covered with a slightly damp cloth. Once prepared, the spring rolls can be cooked immediately or kept covered in the fridge for up to 24 hours.

3 When ready to cook, heat the oil to 180°C. Carefully place the spring rolls into the oil and fry for 3–4 minutes (mini spring rolls), or 4–5 minutes (large spring rolls) or until the spring rolls are golden and crispy. Turn the spring rolls occasionally as they fry.

4 Remove the cooked spring rolls from the oil with tongs or a slotted spoon, draining off any excess oil. Rest on kitchen paper for 1–2 minutes and serve with the sweet-and-sour sauce described on page 110.

Chinese Dipping Sauce (Chinese-takeaway Style)

SERVES 1–2

1½ tablespoons light soy sauce
1½ tablespoons dark soy sauce
1 tablespoon hoisin or barbecue sauce
¼ teaspoon toasted sesame oil
1 garlic clove, finely chopped
¼ teaspoon grated ginger
1 spring onion, finely sliced
Pinch of white sugar

1   In a small bowl, combine the soy sauce, hoisin or barbecue sauce, toasted sesame oil, garlic, ginger, spring onion and sugar, along with 1–2 tablespoons of water. Mix well until thoroughly combined.

2   Place the bowl in the fridge and chill for 1 hour before serving with Prawn Toast (see p.115) or Spring Rolls (p.112).

Prawn Toast (Chinese-takeaway Style)

SERVES 4

350g/12oz raw king prawns
Pinch of Chinese five-spice
Pinch of sea salt
Pinch of white pepper
Pinch of sugar
1 teaspoon oyster sauce mixed with 1 tablespoon water
2 garlic cloves, crushed
Dash of seasoned oil or toasted sesame oil
1 egg, beaten
2 teaspoons Shaoxing rice wine
8 slices of thick white bread
Sesame seeds
Vegetable oil, for deep frying

1   Put the raw king prawns, Chinese five-spice, sea salt, white pepper, sugar, oyster sauce and water, crushed garlic, seasoned oil or toasted sesame oil, egg and rice wine in a blender or food processor. Blitz for 30–40 seconds until you have formed a paste. Spread the paste onto the bread slices.
2   Tip the sesame seeds onto a plate and distribute evenly. Press the bread slices down so that the seeds stick to the prawn paste.
3   When you're ready to cook the toasts, set your deep fryer to 180°C/350°F. Alternatively, fill a wok or large frying pan one third full with vegetable oil and heat to 180°C/350°F. The oil is ready when a few breadcrumbs dropped into the oil sizzle immediately. Deep-fry the prawn toast slices for 2–3 minutes, turning once or twice to ensure both sides are evenly cooked.
4   Remove the prawn toasts from the pan, drain off any excess oil on kitchen paper and cut each slice into 4 triangles. Serve with Sweet Chilli Sauce (see p.165).

Deep-fried Wontons (Chinese-takeaway Style)

SERVES 2
150g/5oz raw prawns, peeled and chopped
½ teaspoon dry sherry
1 teaspoon light soy sauce
2 teaspoons fish sauce
½ teaspoon oyster sauce
Pinch of ground ginger
Pinch of sugar
Dash of toasted sesame oil
6–8 wonton wrappers
Vegetable oil, for deep frying

1   Put the prawns, sherry, soy sauce, fish sauce, oyster sauce, ground ginger, sugar and sesame oil in a large bowl. Mix thoroughly, then cover and refrigerate for 1 hour.
2   Fill the wonton wrappers with a spoonful of the filling and twist the top to seal in the mixture.
3   When you're ready to cook the wontons, set your deep fryer to 180°C/350°F. Alternatively, fill a wok or large frying pan one third full with vegetable oil and heat to 180°C/350°F. The oil is ready when a few breadcrumbs dropped into the oil sizzle immediately. Drop the wontons into the oil over a medium heat for 3–4 minutes, until filling is cooked through and the wrappers are crispy. Drain off any excess oil on kitchen paper and serve with Sweet Chilli Sauce (see p.165).

Beef Chow Mein (Chinese-takeaway Style)

If you're cooking for more than one person, resist the temptation to make a double batch at one time. Instead, cook each portion individually to allow the noodles plenty of heat and space to cook in the pan.

SERVES 1

1 x 200g/7oz sirloin steak
Pinch of garlic powder
Pinch of ground ginger
2 teaspoons vegetable oil
2 teaspoons dark soy sauce mixed with 2 tablespoons Chinese
    Stock (see p.166) or water
½ teaspoon potato flour or cornflour
1 nest of egg noodles
1 onion, sliced
1 large handful beansprouts
1 teaspoon light soy sauce
1–2 spring onions, sliced
Pinch of white pepper
Dash of seasoned oil or toasted sesame oil

1   Trim any excess fat from the sirloin steak and cut the meat into small thin strips.
2   Put the steak strips into a bowl and add the garlic powder, ginger, 1 teaspoon of vegetable oil and 1 teaspoon of the prepared dark soy mixture. Mix well to coat the meat and set aside.
3   Place the egg noodles in a large wok or heat-safe bowl. Cover with boiling water and leave to stand for 3–4 minutes. Use a fork to separate the noodles, then drain and rinse briefly in cold water. Drain again and set aside.

4   Heat a wok or large frying pan over a high heat. Remove the steak from the marinade and stir-fry for 1–2 minutes or until just cooked through. Remove the steak from the pan and set aside.

5   Wipe the pan clean and add the remaining 1 teaspoon of vegetable oil, and heat. Add the sliced onions. Place the beansprouts on top of the onions. Place the noodles on top of the beansprouts. Leave to cook, without stirring, for 1–2 minutes or until the onions begin to smoke at the bottom of the pan.

6   Return the steak slices to the pan. Add the remaining dark soy sauce mixture and allow the liquid to evaporate for 30 seconds. Add the light soy sauce, spring onions and white pepper. Stir-fry thoroughly until all of the noodles are coloured and most of the liquid has evaporated. Add the toasted sesame oil, stir through a final time and serve.

Sirloin Steak (Chinese-takeaway Style)

SERVES 1

1 x 200g/7oz sirloin steak
1 tablespoon vegetable oil
¼ teaspoon sea salt
¼ teaspoon black pepper

FOR THE GRAVY:
2 tablespoons oyster sauce
1 teaspoon light soy sauce
1 teaspoon dark soy sauce
2 teaspoons tomato ketchup
1 teaspoon vegetable oil
½ onion, finely sliced
2–3 button mushrooms, sliced
1 tablespoon Shaoxing rice wine
500ml/17fl oz Chinese Stock (see p.166) or chicken stock
1 heaped teaspoon potato flour or cornflour mixed with
    2 tablespoons water
Dash of seasoned oil or toasted sesame oil

1   First, make the gravy. In a bowl, combine the oyster sauce, light soy
    sauce, dark soy sauce and tomato ketchup.
2   Heat the oil in a large pan over a medium heat. Add the sliced
    onions and mushrooms and stir-fry for 1 minute. Add the rice wine
    and stir-fry for a further 1 minute.
3   Add the prepared bowl of mixed sauces and the stock. Allow the
    mixture to boil for 2–3 minutes until reduced slightly. Lower
    the heat a little and add the potato flour or cornflour mixture,
    stirring well until the gravy thickens. Finish with a dash of
    seasoned oil or toasted sesame oil. Set aside on a low heat until
    needed.

4   Using a meat hammer or the back of a large meat cleaver, hammer the steak thoroughly until thin. Coat the steak with the vegetable oil, and season all over with the sea salt and pepper.

5   Heat a wok or large frying pan over a high heat. Place the steak in the pan and press down gently to ensure even browning. Cook for about 1 minute, turn the steak over and cook for a further 1–2 minutes on the other side, until just cooked through and well browned.

6   Remove the steak from the pan, cover and rest for 1–2 minutes. Top the steak with the gravy and serve with chips or french fries.

Crispy Beef with Sweet Chilli Sauce (Chinese-takeaway Style)

SERVES 1

2 tablespoons Sweet Chilli Sauce (see p.165)
2 tablespoons rice wine vinegar
¼ teaspoon sugar
½ teaspoon light soy sauce
1 x 200g/7oz sirloin steak
1 egg, beaten
8 tablespoons potato flour or cornflour
Vegetable oil, for deep frying, plus extra for stir frying
1 small onion, sliced
½ carrot, sliced into thin strips with a vegetable peeler
1 spring onion, sliced
1 red finger chilli pepper, sliced (optional)
Sea salt and white pepper

1   Put the chilli sauce, rice wine vinegar, sugar and light soy sauce, along with 2 tablespoons of water, in a bowl. Mix well and set aside.
2   Trim any excess fat from the steak and slice the meat into very thin strips, then season the strips well with sea salt and white pepper.
3   Put the beaten egg in one bowl and the potato flour or cornflour in a separate large bowl.
4   Coat the steak slices in the beaten egg, then remove them from the bowl, allowing excess egg to drain off.
5   Drop the egg-coated steak slices into the bowl of potato flour or cornflour and mix well. The steak slices should be completely dry and fully coated in flour.
6   When you're ready to cook the steak, set your deep fryer to 180°C/350°F. Alternatively, fill a wok or large frying pan one third full with vegetable oil and heat to 180°C/350°F. The oil is ready when a few breadcrumbs dropped into the oil sizzle immediately.

Carefully drop the flour-coated steak strips into the oil and fry for around 8 minutes or until crisp. Remove the cooked steak from the pan using a slotted spoon, drain off any excess oil on kitchen paper, and set aside.

7   Heat a wok or large frying pan over a medium heat. Add a touch of oil. Add the onion and carrot and stir-fry for 1–2 minutes. Add the prepared sauce mix and cook for 1 minute.

8   Add the cooked steak slices, spring onion and chilli pepper (if using). Mix through once more and serve with Egg Fried Rice (see p.157).

Mongolian Beef (Chinese-takeaway Style)

SERVES 1

2 tablespoons hoisin sauce

1 teaspoon light soy sauce

1 teaspoon dark soy sauce

4 tablespoons Chinese Stock (see p.166) or water

1 tablespoon Shaoxing rice wine, plus an extra dash (optional)

1 x 200g/7oz sirloin steak

Pinch of potato flour or cornflour

2 teaspoons vegetable oil

¼ red pepper, sliced

4 spring onions, each cut into 4 pieces

Dash of seasoned oil or toasted sesame oil

¼ teaspoon sea salt and ¼ teaspoon white pepper

1   First, make a sauce. In a small bowl, combine the hoisin sauce, light soy sauce, dark soy sauce and stock or water. Add a dash of rice wine, if you wish, then mix well and set aside.

2   Trim any excess fat from the steak and slice into thin strips. Put it in a bowl with the sea salt, white pepper, rice wine and potato or cornflour and mix well. Set aside.

3   Heat 1 teaspoon of the vegetable oil in a wok or large frying pan over a high heat. Tip in the steak slices and cook for 30 seconds to seal on all sides. Stir-fry for a further 1 minute or until just cooked through. Remove from the pan and set aside.

4   Wipe the pan clean and heat the remaining 1 teaspoon of oil over a medium–high heat. Add the red pepper and spring onions. Stir-fry for 1 minute. Return the steak slices to the pan and mix well.

5   Add the prepared sauce to the pan and stir-fry for a further 1–2 minutes or until the sauce begins to thicken. Finish with seasoned oil or toasted sesame oil and serve with Egg Fried Rice (see p.157) or Plain Chow Mein Noodles (p.158).

Singapore-style Chow Mein Noodles (Chinese-takeaway Style)

Cooked chicken, beef, char siu pork or king prawns are perfect additions to this dish. Traditionally made with rice noodles, chow mein is being made more and more using Singapore-style egg noodles.

SERVES 1

1 nest egg noodles
2 teaspoons vegetable oil
1 egg
1 small onion, sliced
2 small green finger chilli peppers, sliced
½ small carrot, peeled into thin strips
1 handful beansprouts
1 tablespoon dark soy sauce
1 teaspoon light soy sauce
½ teaspoon Madras curry powder
2 spring onions, each cut into 4 pieces
Dash of seasoned oil or toasted sesame oil

1   Place the egg noodles in a large wok or heat-safe bowl. Cover with boiling water and set aside for about 4 minutes. Separate the noodles with a fork, drain, rinse briefly with cold water and drain again. Set aside until you're ready to use them.

2   Heat 2 teaspoons of vegetable oil in a wok or large frying pan over a high heat. Crack the egg into the pan and stir-fry for about 30 seconds until the egg is just cooked through and scrambled. Add the onion, chilli peppers, carrots and beansprouts, then tip in the prepared egg noodles.

3   Allow the ingredients to cook over a high heat untouched for about 1 minute. Add the dark soy sauce, light soy sauce and curry powder.

Stir-fry thoroughly for a further 1–2 minutes or until the noodles are evenly coated in sauce and are heated through.

4   Add the spring onion pieces and seasoned oil or toasted sesame oil. Stir through a final time and serve.

Chicken in Tomato (Chinese-takeaway Style)

SERVES 1

1 large skinless, boneless chicken breast fillet (around 115g/4oz weight)

Pinch of potato flour or cornflour mixed with 2 teaspoons of water

3 tablespoons tomato ketchup

1 teaspoon white sugar

1½ teaspoons brown sugar

1 tablespoon white vinegar

½ teaspoon light soy sauce

½ teaspoon dark soy sauce

Pinch of sea salt

2 teaspoons vegetable oil

½ small onion, chopped

1 salad tomato, quartered

1 tablespoon Shaoxing rice wine

1 heaped teaspoon potato flour or cornflour mixed with 1 tablespoon water

1–2 spring onions, sliced

Dash of seasoned oil or toasted sesame oil

1 Trim any excess fat from the chicken breast and cut the meat into small thin strips. Put in a bowl with the potato or cornflour and water mixture. Mix well and set aside.

2 In a bowl, combine the tomato ketchup, white sugar, brown sugar, white vinegar, light soy sauce, dark soy sauce and sea salt, along with 100ml/3½fl oz of water. Mix well and set aside.

3 Heat 1 teaspoon of oil in a wok or large frying pan over a high heat. Add the chicken slices and allow to cook, without stirring, for 1 minute. Then, stir-fry the chicken pieces for 2–3 minutes or until just cooked through. Remove from the pan and set aside.

4   Wipe the wok clean and heat the remaining teaspoon of oil in the pan. Add the onion and tomato. Stir-fry for 1 minute, then add the rice wine. Stir-fry for a further 30 seconds and add the prepared bowl of sauce.

5   Return the chicken to the pan and mix thoroughly. Cook for 1–2 minutes or until the sauce thickens slightly. Thicken further with the heaped teaspoon of potato flour or cornflour mixed with 1 tablespoon of water, mixing well. Add the spring onions. Finish with a dash of seasoned oil or toasted sesame oil and serve with Egg Fried Rice (see p.157).

Szechuan Chicken (Chinese-takeaway Style)

SERVES 1

1 large skinless, boneless chicken breast fillet (around 115g/4oz weight)

Pinch of potato flour or cornflour mixed with 2 teaspoons of water

2 tablespoons apple juice

½ teaspoon Worcestershire sauce

1 teaspoon Tabasco sauce

1 tablespoon toasted sesame oil

¼ teaspoon light soy sauce

¼ teaspoon dark soy sauce

1 tablespoon brown sugar

½ teaspoon dried chilli flakes

Pinch of cayenne pepper

2 teaspoons vegetable oil

1 x 2.5cm/1-inch piece of ginger, finely chopped or grated

1 clove garlic, finely chopped or crushed

½ green pepper, chopped

1 small onion, chopped

1 tablespoon Shaoxing rice wine

1 teaspoon potato flour or cornflour mixed with 1 tablespoon of water

Dash of seasoned oil or toasted sesame oil

1 Trim any excess fat from the chicken breast and cut the meat into small thin strips. Put in a bowl with the the pinch of potato or cornflour mixed with 2 teaspoons of water. Mix well and set aside.

2 In a bowl, make a sauce by combining apple juice, Worcestershire sauce, Tabasco sauce, toasted sesame oil, light soy sauce, dark soy sauce, brown sugar, chilli flakes and cayenne pepper, along with 3–4 tablespoons of water. Mix well and set aside.

3 Heat 1 teaspoon of oil in a wok or large frying pan over a high heat. Add the chicken slices and allow to cook, without stirring, for 1 minute. Then, stir-fry the chicken pieces for 2–3 minutes or until just cooked through. Remove from the pan and set aside.

4 Wipe the wok clean and heat the remaining teaspoon of oil in the pan. Add the green pepper and onion. Stir fry for 1–2 minutes, then add the rice wine. Stir-fry for a further 30 seconds and add the prepared bowl of sauce.

5 Return the chicken to the pan and mix thoroughly. Cook for 1–2 minutes or until the sauce thickens slightly. Thicken further with the 1 teaspoon of potato or cornflour mixed with 1 tablespoon of water, mixing well. Finish with a dash of seasoned oil or toasted sesame oil and serve with Egg Fried Rice (see p.157).

Chicken in Black Pepper Sauce (Chinese-takeaway Style)

SERVES 1

1 large skinless, boneless chicken breast fillet (about 115g/4oz weight)
Pinch of potato flour or cornflour mixed with 2 teaspoons of water
3 tablespoons oyster sauce
½ teaspoon light soy sauce
1 teaspoon black pepper
½ teaspoon white pepper
1 teaspoon sake
100ml/3½fl oz Chinese Stock (see p.166) or water
2 teaspoons of vegetable oil
1 small onion, chopped
½ red pepper, chopped
½ green pepper, chopped
1 teaspoon of potato flour or cornflour mixed with 1 tablespoon of water
Dash of seasoned oil or toasted sesame oil

1   Trim any excess fat from the chicken breast and cut the meat into small thin strips. Put in a bowl and add the pinch of potato flour or cornflour and 2 teaspoons of water. Mix well and set aside.

2   In a bowl, make a sauce by combining the oyster sauce, light soy sauce, black pepper, white pepper, sake and water or Chinese stock. Mix well and set aside.

3   Heat 1 teaspoon of oil in a wok or large frying pan over a high heat. Add the chicken slices and allow to cook, without stirring, for 1 minute. Then, stir-fry the chicken pieces for a 1–2 minutes or until just cooked through. Remove from the pan and set aside.

4   Wipe the wok clean and heat the remaining teaspoon of oil in the pan. Add the onion, red pepper and green pepper. Stir-fry for 1–2 minutes. Add the prepared sauce and mix well.

5 Return the chicken to the pan. Cook for 1–2 minutes or until the sauce thickens slightly. Reduce the heat slightly and thicken further with the 1 teaspoon of potato flour or cornflour mixed with 1 tablespoon of water, mixing well. Finish with a dash of seasoned oil or toasted sesame oil and serve with Egg Fried Rice (see p.157).

Kung Pao Chicken (Chinese-takeaway Style)

SERVES 1

1 tablespoon Shaoxing rice wine

1 teaspoon rice wine vinegar

1 teaspoon light soy sauce

1 teaspoon dark soy sauce

½ teaspoon toasted sesame oil

1 teaspoon sugar

2 tablespoons Chinese Stock (see p.166) or water

½ teaspoon potato flour or cornflour

1 large chicken breast (around 115g/4oz weight)

2 teaspoons vegetable oil

¼ red pepper, chopped

¼ green pepper, chopped

½ small onion, chopped

1 dried red chilli pepper

1 teaspoon Garlic & Ginger Paste (see p.217)

2 tablespoons roasted peanuts

1 In a bowl, make a sauce by combining the rice wine, rice wine vinegar, light soy sauce, dark soy sauce, toasted sesame oil, sugar, stock or water, and potato flour or cornflour. Mix well and set aside.

2 Trim any excess fat from the chicken breast and cut the meat into thin strips. Put it in a bowl and add 1 tablespoon of the prepared sauce and mix well.

3 Heat 1 teaspoon of vegetable oil in a wok or large frying pan over a high heat. Add the chicken slices and leave, without stirring, for 30 seconds to seal. Then, stir-fry the chicken for 2–3 minutes or until just cooked through. Remove and set aside.

4 Wipe out the pan and heat the remaining 1 teaspoon of oil. Add the red pepper, green pepper, onion and dried red chilli. Stir-fry for 1

minute. Add the garlic and ginger paste and stir-fry for a further 1 minute.

5   Return the chicken to the pan and add the prepared sauce. Mix well and cook for a further 1 minute or until the sauce begins to thicken. Top with roasted peanuts and serve with Egg Fried Rice (see p.157) or Plain Chow Mein Noodles (p.158)

Breast of Chicken Peking Style
(Chinese-takeaway Style)

SERVES 1

2 tablespoons Worcestershire sauce

3 tablespoons tomato ketchup

1 tablespoon Coleman's OK sauce, or brown sauce

1 teaspoon Sweet Chilli Sauce (see p.165)

1 teaspoon light soy sauce

1 teaspoon dark soy sauce

1 teaspoon rice wine vinegar

¼ teaspoon sugar

Large pinch of Chinese 5-spice

1 large skinless, boneless chicken breast fillet (about 115g/4oz
    weight)

2 teaspoons vegetable oil

½ green pepper, chopped

1 onion, chopped

1 teaspoon potato flour or cornflour mixed with 2 tablespoons
    water, plus an extra pinch of the flour

Dash of seasoned oil or toasted sesame oil

1   In a bowl, make a sauce by combining the Worcestershire sauce,
    tomato ketchup, OK or brown sauce, sweet chilli sauce, light soy
    sauce, dark soy sauce, rice wine vinegar, sugar, Chinese five-spice
    and 75ml/2¼fl oz of water. Mix well and set aside.

2   Trim any excess fat from the chicken breast and cut the meat into
    thin slices. Put in a bowl and add 1 tablespoon of the prepared sauce
    and a pinch of potato flour or cornflour and mix well.

3   Heat 1 teaspoon of vegetable oil in a wok or large frying pan
    over a high heat. Add the chicken slices and leave for 30 seconds to
    seal. Stir-fry the chicken for 2–3 minutes or until just cooked
    through. Remove and set aside.

4   Wipe the pan clean and add the remaining 1 teaspoon of oil. Add the green pepper and onion, then stir-fry for 1 minute. Add the remaining prepared sauce and mix well.

5   Return the chicken to the pan. Cook for 1–2 minutes to thicken the sauce a little. Reduce the heat slightly and add the 1 teaspoon of potato flour or cornflour mixed with 1 tablespoon of water, mixing well so that the sauce continues to thicken. Finish with a dash of seasoned oil or toasted sesame oil and serve with Egg Fried Rice (see p.157).

Chicken Mushroom (Chinese-takeaway Style)

Deep frying the mushrooms offers the most authentic results in this dish. However, if you prefer you can stir-fry them in just a little oil for 3–4 minutes.

SERVES 1
1 tablespoon oyster sauce
½ teaspoon light soy sauce
½ teaspoon dark soy sauce
50ml/1½fl oz Chinese Stock (see p.166) or water
Pinch of white pepper
1 large skinless, boneless chicken breast (about 115g/4oz weight)
2 teaspoons vegetable oil, plus extra for deep frying
5–6 button mushrooms, halved
1 small onion, chopped
1 tablespoon Shaoxing rice wine
1 teaspoon potato flour or cornflour mixed with 2 tablespoons
    water, plus an extra pinch of the flour
Dash of seasoned oil or toasted sesame oil

1   In a bowl, make a sauce by combining the oyster sauce, light soy sauce, dark soy sauce, Chinese Stock or water and white pepper. Set aside.

2   Trim any excess fat from the chicken breast and cut the meat into thin slices. Put in a bowl and add 1 teaspoon of the prepared sauce and a pinch of potato flour or cornflour. Mix well.

3   Heat 1 teaspoon of the vegetable oil in a wok or large frying pan over a high heat. Add the chicken slices and leave for 30 seconds to seal. Stir-fry for about 2–3 minutes or until just cooked through. Remove and set aside.

4   When you're ready to cook the chicken, set your deep fryer to 180°C/350°F. Alternatively, fill a wok or large frying pan one third

full with vegetable oil and heat to 180°C/350°F. The oil is ready when a few breadcrumbs dropped into the oil sizzle immediately. Deep-fry the mushrooms for about 20–30 seconds. Remove the mushrooms from the pan, drain off any excess oil and set aside.

5   Wipe out the wok or frying pan and heat the remaining 1 teaspoon of vegetable oil over a high heat. Add the onion and cooked mushrooms to the pan and stir-fry for about 1 minute. Add the rice wine and cook for a further 30 seconds. Add the prepared sauce and mix well.

6   Return the chicken to the pan. Cook for 1–2 minutes or until the sauce thickens a little. Reduce the heat slightly and add the 1 teaspoon of potato flour or cornflour mixed with 2 tablespoons of water, mixing well, until the sauce thickens some more. Finish with a dash of seasoned oil or toasted sesame oil and serve with Egg Fried Rice (see p.157).

Shredded Crispy Chicken with Sweet Chilli Sauce (Chinese-takeaway Style)

SERVES 1

2 tablespoons Sweet Chilli Sauce (see p.165)

2 tablespoons rice wine vinegar

¼ teaspoon sugar

½ teaspoon light soy sauce

1 egg, beaten

8 tablespoons potato flour or cornflour

1 large skinless, boneless chicken breast fillet (around 115g/4oz weight)

1 teaspoon vegetable oil, plus extra for deep frying

½ small onion, chopped

¼ green pepper, chopped

¼ small carrot, peeled into thin strips

1   In a bowl make a sauce by combining the sweet chilli sauce, rice wine vinegar, sugar and light soy sauce, along with 2 tablespoons of water. Mix well and set aside.

2   Trim any excess fat from the chicken breast and cut the meat into small bite-sized pieces.

3   Put the beaten egg into one large bowl and the potato flour or cornflour into another.

4   Drop the chicken pieces into the beaten egg. Mix well to coat, then lift them out with your hands, allowing the excess egg to fall back into the bowl.

5   Drop the egg-coated chicken pieces into the bowl of potato flour or cornflour and coat well. The chicken pieces should become completely dry and fully coated in flour.

6   When you're ready to cook the chicken, set your deep fryer to 180°C/350°F. Alternatively, fill a wok or large frying pan one third

full with vegetable oil and heat to 180°C/350°F. The oil is ready when a few breadcrumbs dropped into the oil sizzle immediately. Carefully drop the flour-coated chicken pieces into the oil and deep-fry for about 4–5 minutes or until cooked through, golden and crispy. Remove the chicken pieces from the pan using a slotted spoon and drain off any excess oil on kitchen paper.

7   In a wok or large frying pan, heat 1 teaspoon of vegetable oil. Add the vegetables and stir-fry for about 1–2 minutes. Add the prepared sauce and mix well. Cook for a further 30 seconds until the sauce becomes slightly thick.

8   Add the cooked crispy chicken pieces, mix well and serve with Egg Fried Rice (see p.157) or Plain Chow Mein Noodles (p.158).

Chicken Balls with Sweet & Sour Sauce (Chinese-takeaway Style)

SERVES 1–2

60ml/2fl oz tomato ketchup
20ml/1fl oz white vinegar
¼ teaspoon light soy sauce
70g/2½oz white sugar, plus ¼ teaspoon
35g/1¼oz brown sugar
1½ tablespoons potato flour or cornflour mixed with 2 tablespoons
    water, plus an extra pinch of the flour
250g/9oz self-raising flour
1 large skinless, boneless chicken breast fillet (around 115g/4oz
    weight)
½ teaspoon seasoned oil or toasted sesame oil
Vegetable oil, for deep frying
Sea salt and white pepper

1   In a small pan, combine the tomato ketchup, white vinegar, light soy
    sauce, the 70g/2½oz white sugar, and the brown sugar, along with
    70ml/2½fl oz of water. Mix well and bring to the boil. Allow to
    simmer for 1–2 minutes.
2   Add the potato flour or cornflour and water mixture, stir well and
    cook for a further 2 minutes until you have a thick and syrupy
    sauce. Pour the sauce into a large serving bowl and set aside.
3   In a large bowl, combine the self-raising flour, ½ teaspoon of sea
    salt, the ¼ teaspoon of white sugar and a pinch of white pepper,
    along with 250ml/9fl oz of water. Mix well into a thick batter.
4   Trim any excess fat from the chicken breast and cut the meat into
    7–8 bite-sized pieces. Add a pinch of sea salt, pinch of white pepper,
    pinch of potato flour or cornflour and the seasoned oil or toasted
    sesame oil. Mix well.
5   When you're ready to cook the chicken, set your deep fryer to
    180°C/350°F. Alternatively, fill a wok or large frying pan one third

full with vegetable oil and heat to 180°C/350°F. The oil is ready when a few breadcrumbs dropped into the oil sizzle immediately. Dip the chicken pieces into the batter and then drop them carefully into the hot oil. Fry for 4–5 minutes or until the batter is golden and the chicken balls are cooked through.

6 Remove the chicken balls from the pan using a slotted spoon, drain off any excess oil on kitchen paper and serve with the sauce alongside.

Chicken in Salt & Chilli (Chinese-takeaway Style)

SERVES 1

1 large skinless, boneless chicken breast (about 115g/4oz weight)
1 teaspoon Shaoxing rice wine
Dash of toasted sesame oil
1 egg, beaten
6 tablespoons potato flour or cornflour
1 teaspoon vegetable oil, plus extra for deep frying
½ green pepper, sliced
½ small onion, sliced
1–2 green finger chilli peppers, sliced
2 garlic cloves, finely sliced or crushed
3 spring onions, finely sliced
½–1 teaspoon Sea Salt & Szechuan Seasoning (see p.163)
1 tablespoon Shaoxing rice wine
Dash of seasoned oil or extra dash toasted sesame oil
Sea salt and white pepper

1   Trim any excess fat from the chicken breast and cut the meat into
    7–8 small pieces. Add the teaspoon of rice wine and sesame oil, and
    season with a pinch each of sea salt and white pepper. Mix well and
    set aside.

2   Put the beaten egg in one large bowl and the potato flour or
    cornflour in another.

3   Drop the chicken pieces into the egg. Mix well to coat, then lift out
    the chicken pieces with your hands, allowing any excess egg to fall
    back into the bowl.

4   Drop the egg-coated chicken pieces into the potato flour or
    cornflour and mix well. The chicken pieces should become
    completely dry and fully coated in flour.

5   When you're ready to cook the chicken, set your deep fryer to
    180°C/350°F. Alternatively, fill a wok or large frying pan one third

full with vegetable oil and heat to 180°C/350°F. The oil is ready when a few breadcrumbs dropped into the oil sizzle immediately. Carefully drop the flour-coated chicken pieces into the oil and fry for around 4–5 minutes or until cooked through, golden and crispy. Remove the chicken pieces from the pan using a slotted spoon and drain off any excess oil on kitchen paper.

6 In a wok or large frying pan, heat the teaspoon of vegetable oil over a medium heat. Add the green pepper, onion, chilli peppers, garlic and spring onions and stir-fry for about 1–2 minutes or until fragrant. Add the sea salt & chilli seasoning to taste (be generous) and mix well. Add the 1 tablespoon of Shaoxing rice wine, mix well once more and finish with just a touch of seasoned oil or toasted sesame oil. Serve with Sweet Chilli Sauce (see p.165) or Sweet & Sour Dipping Sauce (p.164) on the side.

Chicken Skewers with Satay Sauce (Chinese-takeaway Style)

You'll need four skewers for this recipe. If you're using wooden ones, soak them in water for 30 minutes before cooking, to prevent them from burning.

SERVES 1–2 (MAKES 4 SKEWERS)
2 tablespoons vegetable oil
½ small onion, finely chopped
1 teaspoon mild Madras curry powder, plus an extra pinch
3 tablespoons peanut butter
1 teaspoon light soy sauce
1 teaspoon dark soy sauce
200ml/7fl oz coconut milk
1 tablespoon brown sugar
Pinch of dried chilli flakes
1 large skinless, boneless chicken breast fillet (around 115g/4oz weight)
Pinch of ground coriander
Pinch of turmeric
Pinch of potato flour or cornflour

1   In a small saucepan or frying pan, heat 1 tablespoon of the vegetable oil over a low–medium heat. Add the chopped onion and stir-fry for 1–2 minutes or until just beginning to soften. Add the teaspoon of curry powder and stir-fry for 1 minute. Add the peanut butter and stir-fry for a further 1 minute or until the peanut butter is just beginning to melt.

2   Add the light soy sauce, dark soy sauce, coconut milk, brown sugar and dried chilli flakes, along with 75ml/2½fl oz of water. Bring to the boil and simmer on a low heat until the sauce is combined and you reach the desired consistency. Remove from the heat and set aside. The sauce will thicken upon cooling and can be reheated when needed, adding a little water if necessary.

3   Trim any excess fat from the chicken breast and cut the meat into 6–8 long thin slices. Put them in a bowl with a pinch of curry powder, and the ground coriander, turmeric, potato flour or cornflour, remaining vegetable oil and 1 teaspoon of water. Mix well and set aside to marinate for 10 minutes.

4   Preheat the grill to high.

5   Thread the chicken strips onto the skewers, threading in and out of each strip so that you pierce each one several times. Each skewer should comfortably hold two strips of chicken.

6   Grill the skewered chicken on a high heat for about 2–3 minutes each side, or until the chicken is cooked through and just beginning to char. The chicken skewers also cook very well on a double-plated health grill for about 5–6 minutes.

7   Remove the cooked chicken skewers and arrange on a serving dish. Drizzle with the prepared sauce and serve with Egg Fried Rice (see p.157)

Sweet-&-Sour Pork Hong-Kong Style (Chinese-takeaway Style)

SERVES 1

3 tablespoons tomato ketchup

1 teaspoon white sugar

1½ teaspoons brown sugar

2 tablespoons rice wine vinegar

½ teaspoon light soy sauce

½ teaspoon dark soy sauce

1 large pork loin steak (about 115g/4oz weight)

1 egg, beaten

6 tablespoons potato flour or cornflour

Vegetable oil, for frying

¼ red pepper, chopped

¼ green pepper, chopped

1 small onion, chopped

1 tinned pineapple ring, chopped

1 teaspoon potato flour or cornflour mixed with 2 tablespoons water

Sea salt and white pepper

1   In a bowl, make a sweet-and-sour sauce by combining tomato ketchup, white sugar, brown sugar, rice wine vinegar, light soy sauce, dark soy sauce, along with 100ml/3½fl oz of water. Mix well and set aside.

2   Trim any excess fat from the pork and cut the meat into 7–8 small pieces. Put in a bowl and season with a pinch each of sea salt and white pepper. Mix well and set aside.

3   Put the beaten egg in one large bowl, and the potato flour or cornflour in another large bowl.

4   Drop the pork pieces into the egg. Mix well, then lift the pork pieces out of the bowl with your hands, allowing excess egg to fall back into the bowl.

5 Drop the egg-coated pork pieces into the bowl of potato flour or cornflour and mix well. The pork pieces should become completely dry and fully coated in flour.

6 When you're ready to cook the pork, set your deep fryer to 180°C/350°F. Alternatively, fill a wok or large frying pan one third full with vegetable oil and heat to 180°C/350°F. The oil is ready when a few breadcrumbs dropped into the oil sizzle immediately. Carefully drop the flour-coated pork pieces into the oil and fry for about 3–4 minutes or until cooked through, golden and crispy. Remove the pork pieces from the pan and drain off any excess oil.

7 Heat 1 teaspoon of oil in a wok or large frying pan over a high heat. Add the red pepper, green pepper, onion and pineapple. Stir-fry for 1 minute, then add the prepared sauce. Cook for a further 2 minutes or until the sauce begins to thicken. Lower the heat a little and thicken further with potato flour or cornflour and water mixture, mixing well.

8 Add the cooked crispy pork and mix thoroughly. Serve with Egg Fried Rice (see p.157).

Char Siu Chinese Roast Pork (Chinese-takeaway Style)

If you prefer you could slice the marinated pork fillet into long thin strips and grill the strips on skewers to create individual char siu kebabs.

SERVES 3–4

1 tablespoon honey
1 tablespoon rice wine
2 teaspoons soy sauce
3 tablespoons hoisin or barbecue sauce
2 tablespoons tomato ketchup
1 teaspoon toasted sesame oil
¼ teaspoon Chinese five-spice powder
½ teaspoon garlic powder
¼ teaspoon ground ginger
About 500g/1lb 2oz pork fillet

1   In a bowl, make a marinade by combining the honey, rice wine, soy sauce, hoisin or barbecue sauce, tomato ketchup, toasted sesame oil, Chinese five-spice, garlic powder and ground ginger, along with 3–4 tablespoons of water.
2   Add the pork fillet and rub the marinade thoroughly into the meat, then cover the bowl and place in the fridge to marinate for at least 4 hours or overnight if possible, turning the pork fillet occasionally.
3   Preheat the oven to 200°C/400°F/Gas Mark 6.
4   Pour 100ml/3½fl oz of water into a roasting tray and place the marinated pork fillet on a rack above the tray, reserving any leftover marinade. Place the pork into the hot oven and roast for 40–45 minutes or until cooked through. When the char siu is cooked, remove from the oven and rest for 4–5 minutes, then transfer to a serving dish and cut into slices.

5   To create a sauce or glaze for the dish, put any leftover marinade in a small saucepan and bring to the boil. Reduce the heat to low and simmer for 2–3 minutes. Pour the simmering marinade over the sliced char siu and serve with Egg Fried Rice (see p.157).

Crispy Pork Balls (Chinese-takeaway Style)

SERVES 1–2

250g/9oz self-raising flour
¼ teaspoon white sugar
2 pork loin steaks (each about 115g/4oz weight)
Pinch of potato flour or cornflour
½ teaspoon toasted sesame oil
Vegetable oil, for deep frying
Sea salt and white pepper

1   In a large bowl, combine the self-raising flour and white sugar with
    250ml/9fl oz of water and ½ teaspoon of sea salt. Mix well into a
    thick batter.
2   Trim any excess fat from the pork steaks and cut each steak into 7–8
    bite-sized pieces. Put in a bowl with the potato flour or cornflour and
    toasted sesame oil, and season with a pinch of sea salt and white
    pepper. Mix well.
3   When you're ready to cook the pork balls, set your deep fryer to
    180°C/350°F. Alternatively, fill a wok or large frying pan one third
    full with vegetable oil and heat to 180°C/350°F. The oil is ready
    when a few breadcrumbs dropped into the oil sizzle immediately.
    Dip the pork pieces into the batter and then drop carefully into the
    hot oil. Fry for 4–5 minutes or until the batter is golden and the
    pork balls are cooked through.
4   Remove the pork balls from the pan, drain off any excess oil and
    serve with Sweet Chilli Sauce (see p.165) or Sweet & Sour Dipping
    Sauce (p.164) on the side.

King Prawn with Ginger & Spring Onion (Chinese-takeaway Style)

SERVES 1

150g/5½oz raw king prawns
Pinch of potato flour or cornflour mixed with 1 tablespoon water
2 teaspoons vegetable oil
½ small onion, sliced
2–3 spring onions, each cut into 4 pieces
1 tablespoon Shaoxing rice wine
1 garlic clove, finely chopped or crushed
2.5cm/1-inch piece of ginger, roughly sliced
1 tablespoon oyster sauce
½ teaspoon light soy sauce
½ teaspoon dark soy sauce
75ml/2¼fl oz Chinese Stock (see p.166) or chicken stock
Pinch of sugar
1 heaped teaspoon potato flour or cornflour mixed with 2
    tablespoons water
Dash of seasoned oil or toasted sesame oil
Sea salt and white pepper

1   In a large bowl, combine the king prawns and the pinch of potato
     flour or cornflour and 1 tablespoon of water. Mix well and set aside.
2   Heat 1 teaspoon of vegetable oil in a wok or large frying pan over a
     high heat. Add the king prawns and allow to seal for 30 seconds,
     then stir-fry for 2–3 minutes or until the prawns are pink and
     cooked through. Remove and set aside.
3   Wipe the pan clean and heat the remaining 1 teaspoon of vegetable
     oil over a high heat. Add the onion and spring onions. Stir-fry for
     30 seconds. Add the Shaoxing rice wine and stir-fry for a further
     30 seconds.
4   Add the garlic and ginger and stir-fry for a further 30 seconds, then
     add the oyster sauce, dark soy sauce, stock, a pinch of sea salt and

sugar and season with a pinch of white pepper. Mix well and cook for a further 2 minutes or until the sauce begins to thicken. Lower the heat a little and thicken further with the 1 heaped teaspoon of potato flour or cornflour mixed with 2 tablespoons of water, mixing well.

5   Return the cooked king prawns to the pan, stir to combine, then finish with a dash of seasoned oil or toasted sesame oil and serve with Egg Fried Rice (see p.157) or Plain Chow Mein Noodles (p.158).

Mixed Vegetable Chop Suey (Chinese-takeaway Style)

SERVES 1

2 tablespoons oyster sauce

½ teaspoon light soy sauce

½ teaspoon dark soy sauce

¼ teaspoon sugar

100ml/3½fl oz vegetable stock or water

1 tablespoon vegetable oil

1 onion, chopped

½ red pepper, chopped

½ green pepper, chopped

3–4 broccoli florets, chopped

3–4 button mushrooms, sliced

1 small handful shredded pak choi or green cabbage

1 small handful beansprouts

1 tablespoon Shaoxing rice wine

Pinch of white pepper

1 teaspoon potato flour or cornflour mixed with 2 tablespoons water

Dash of seasoned oil or toasted sesame oil

1   In a bowl, make a sauce by combining the oyster sauce, light soy sauce, dark soy sauce, sugar and vegetable stock or water. Mix well and set aside.

2   Heat the vegetable oil in a wok or large frying pan over a high heat. Add the onion, red pepper, green pepper, broccoli, mushrooms, pak choi or cabbage and beansprouts. Stir-fry for 3–4 minutes. Add the rice wine and white pepper and stir-fry for a further 30 seconds.

3   Add the prepared sauce, mix well and cook for a further 2 minutes or until the sauce begins to thicken. Lower the heat a little and thicken further with the potato or cornflour and water mixture, mixing well.

4   Finish with a dash of seasoned oil or toasted sesame oil and serve
    with Egg Fried Rice (see p.157) or Plain Chow Mein Noodles
    (p.158).

Mushroom Omelette

A well-seasoned or non-stick wok helps greatly in making omelettes and is well worth the investment.

SERVES 1
1 tablespoon vegetable oil, plus extra for stir frying
4 small button mushrooms, sliced
2 eggs
½ teaspoon toasted sesame oil
¼ teaspoon sea salt

1 Heat a little vegetable oil in the wok over a high heat. Add the sliced mushrooms and stir-fry for 2–3 minutes or until cooked. Remove and set aside.

2 Crack the eggs into a small bowl and add toasted sesame oil. Whisk to combine thoroughly.

3 Add the tablespoon of vegetable oil to the wok over a high heat. Reduce the heat to medium and pour the egg mixture into the wok. Add the cooked mushrooms and tilt the pan to ensure uncooked egg runs to the side of the pan. Shake the pan around in a circular motion. Use a ladle to hold the mushroom and cooked egg mixture in the middle of the pan and tilt the pan once again. Any uncooked egg mixture will run to the side of the pan.

4 Continue to shake the pan in a circular motion so that the egg stays together. Season with sea salt and increase the heat to medium–high. Using one swift motion, flip the omelette over in the pan. This may take some practice – you'll find it easier if you have a well-shaped wok and over high heat.

5 Press down on the omelette with the ladle in order to help the omelette brown evenly. Flip the egg again a few times until completely cooked – it should take 2–3 minutes altogether. Fold the mushroom omelette and serve in a long foil tray for added takeaway authenticity.

Boiled Rice (Chinese-takeaway Style)

You can scale up the portions, but always use the same proportions – 200ml/7fl oz of water for every 100g/3½oz of rice.

SERVES 1
100g/3½oz good-quality basmati rice per portion (uncooked weight)

1   Place the basmati rice in a large bowl and cover with plenty of cold water. After 10 minutes, drain and re-cover the rice. Repeat every 10 minutes for 30–40 minutes.
2   Tip the rice into a colander and rinse for a final time under running water until the water runs clear, then place the rice into a large pan. Cover with 200ml/7fl oz of water (the amount is important) and bring the boil over a high heat.
3   When the rice starts to boil, place the lid on the plan, reduce the heat to the lowest setting and cook untouched for 14 minutes. Switch off the heat and allow the rice to stand for a further 10 minutes.
4   Serve immediately with any Chinese meal, or cool it quickly and store in an airtight container in the fridge overnight and make Egg Fried Rice (see p.157).

NOTE: Refrigerate cooked and cooled rice immediately. It's not safe to consume rice that has been resting at room temperature for too long.

Egg Fried Rice (Chinese-takeaway Style)

SERVES 1–2

2 teaspoons vegetable oil

1 egg

1 portion cooked and cooled basmati rice (see p.156)

1½ teaspoons light soy sauce

1½ teaspoons dark soy sauce

1 handful chopped spring onions (optional)

Dash of seasoned oil or toasted sesame oil

Sea salt and white pepper

1 Heat the oil in a wok or large frying pan over a high heat. Crack the egg into the pan and stir-fry for 30 seconds until just cooked and broken up.

2 Add the basmati rice to the pan, lower the heat to medium and mix well. Stir fry the rice for 2 minutes.

3 Add the light soy sauce and dark soy sauce, and season with sea salt and pepper. Stir fry for a further 1 minute, then add the chopped spring onions, if using. Increase the heat to high and stir-fry for a further 1 minute.

4 Finish with a dash of seasoned oil or toasted sesame oil and serve with any Chinese meal.

Plain Chow Mein Noodles (Chinese-takeaway Style)

SERVES 1–2

1 nest egg noodles
2 teaspoons vegetable oil
1 small onion, sliced
1 large handful beansprouts
1 tablespoon dark soy sauce mixed with 3 tablespoons water
1 teaspoon light soy sauce
Pinch of white pepper
1–2 spring onions, sliced
Dash of seasoned oil or toasted sesame oil

1   Place the egg noodles in a large wok or heat-safe bowl. Cover with boiling water and set aside for about 4 minutes. Separate the noodles with a fork, drain, rinse briefly with cold water and drain again. Set aside.

2   Heat the vegetable oil in a wok or large frying pan over a high heat. Add the onions. Place the beansprouts on top of the onions, and the noodles on top of the beansprouts.

3   Allow the ingredients to cook over a high heat untouched for about 1 minute. Add the dark soy sauce and water mixture and allow to cook untouched for a further 1 minute.

4   Add the light soy sauce, white pepper and spring onions. Stir-fry for a further 1–2 minutes or until the noodles are evenly coated in sauce and are heated through.

5   Add the seasoned oil or toasted sesame oil. Stir through a final time and serve with any Chinese meal.

Salt & Pepper Chips (Chinese-takeaway Style)

You'll find exactly the chips you need for this recipe in the frozen section of your nearest Chinese supermarket, however any inexpensive potato chips or fries will work well.

SERVES 1–2

1 large portion frozen chips
1 tablespoon vegetable oil
½ red pepper, finely chopped
½ green pepper, finely chopped
1 small onion, finely chopped
2 spring onions, sliced
2 green finger chilli peppers, finely sliced
2 garlic cloves, finely chopped or crushed
Sea Salt & Szechuan Seasoning (see p.163), to taste
1 tablespoon Shaoxing rice wine
Dash of seasoned oil or toasted sesame oil

1   Cook the chips according to the packet instructions.
2   When they are almost cooked, heat the vegetable oil in a wok or large frying pan over a medium heat. Add the red pepper, green pepper, onion, spring onions, chilli peppers and garlic and stir-fry for 1–2 minutes.
3   When the chips are ready, add them to the pan. Season generously with the sea salt & pepper seasoning and mix well.
4   Add the rice wine and stir-fry for a further 30 seconds, then finish with a dash of seasoned oil or toasted sesame oil and serve.

French Fried Onion Rings
(Chinese-takeaway Style)

SERVES 1–2
250g/9oz self-raising flour
Pinch of sugar
1 large Spanish onion, sliced
Vegetable oil, for deep frying
Sea salt

1   In a large bowl, combine the self-raising flour and sugar with
    250ml/9fl oz of water and season with a pinch of sea salt. Mix well
    to a thick batter.
2   Season the onion slices with a little sea salt and add to the bowl of
    batter.
3   When you're ready to cook the onion rings, set your deep fryer to
    180°C/350°F. Alternatively, fill a wok or large frying pan one third
    full with vegetable oil and heat to 180°C/350°F. The oil is ready
    when a few breadcrumbs dropped into the oil sizzle immediately.
    Carefully ensure each onion ring is coated in batter and one by one,
    drop the coated rings into the oil. Fry in batches for around 3–4
    minutes or until the batter is golden and crispy.
4   Remove the onion rings from the pan using a slotted spoon and
    drain off any excess oil on kitchen paper. Season with a little sea
    salt and serve with Sweet & Sour Dipping Sauce (see p.164).

Crispy Seaweed (Chinese-takeaway Style)

SERVES 1
7–8 large cabbage, pak choi or spring green leaves
Vegetable oil, for deep frying
½ teaspoon sugar
Sea salt

1   Preheat the oven to 150°C/300°F/Gas Mark 2.
2   Remove the stalks from the cabbage or spring green leaves. Roll the leaves up and shred into fine strips. Wash the strips in cold water, then pat dry with kitchen paper.
3   Arrange the shredded leaves on a baking tray and place in the oven a for about 12 minutes. Remove from the oven and set aside until ready for use. The dried leaves will keep well in a sealed container for up to 24 hours.
4   When you're ready to cook the seaweed, set your deep fryer to 180°C/350°F. Alternatively, fill a wok or large frying pan one third full with vegetable oil and heat to 180°C/350°F. The oil is ready when a few breadcrumbs dropped into the oil sizzle immediately. Carefully drop the leaves into the oil. Fry for about 30 seconds or until crisp. Remove the leaves from the pan using a spider or slotted spoon. Drain off any excess oil on kitchen paper and toss the leaves in the sugar mixed with a pinch of sea salt. Serve with any Chinese dish.

Salt & Chilli Seasoning (Chinese-takeaway Style)

1 tablespoon sea salt
½ tablespoon sugar
¼ tablespoon Chinese five-spice
1–2 teaspoons dried crushed chilli flakes
¼ teaspoon garlic powder
Pinch of ground ginger
Pinch of white pepper

1 Mix together all the ingredients thoroughly and store in a sealed container until needed.

Sea Salt & Szechuan Seasoning (Chinese-takeaway Style)

Makes 1 small tub of sea salt and pepper seasoning, enough for around 4–6 portions of Chicken in Salt & Chilli (see p.142).

1 tablespoon sea salt
1½ teaspoons ground Szechuan pepper
¼ teaspoon black pepper
Pinch of white pepper
¼ teaspoon Chinese five-spice
Pinch of chilli powder

1 In a small bowl, add the sea salt, Szechuan pepper, black pepper, white pepper, Chinese five-spice and chilli powder and mix thoroughly.
2 The prepared sea salt-and-pepper mixture will keep well for up to 1 month and can be used to season pork ribs, chips and chicken.

Sweet & Sour Dipping Sauce (Chinese-takeaway Style)

SERVES 1

3 tablespoons tomato ketchup
½ teaspoon light soy sauce
½ teaspoon dark soy sauce
½ teaspoon white sugar
1½ teaspoons brown sugar
1 tablespoon white vinegar
1 teaspoon potato flour or cornflour mixed with 2 tablespoons
    water

1   In a small pan, combine the tomato ketchup, light soy sauce, dark
    soy sauce, white sugar, brown sugar, white vinegar and 100ml of
    water. Bring to the boil and simmer for around 2 minutes.
2   Lower the heat slightly and add the potato flour or cornflour and
    water mixture, stirring thoroughly. Cook for a further 1–2 minutes
    until the sauce is thickened and serve immediately or set aside to
    cool and serve with Chicken in Salt & Chilli (see p.142).

Sweet Chilli Sauce (Chinese-takeaway Style)

Sweet and spicy, this sauce makes a great dip or accompaniment to various Chinese dishes.

MAKES AROUND 200ML/7FL OZ SAUCE
2 tablespoons dry sherry
2 tablespoons fish sauce
100ml/4fl oz rice wine vinegar
150g/5oz white sugar
2–4 teaspoons chilli flakes
1 tablespoon potato or cornflour mixed with 2 tablespoons water

1 In a small pan, combine the sherry, fish sauce, rice wine vinegar, sugar and chilli flakes, along with 50ml/2fl oz of water.
2 Put the pan on a high heat and bring to the boil, then reduce the heat to medium–low and simmer for 8–10 minutes or until the sauce is reduced.
3 Add the cornflour mixture to the sauce and stir to combine. Allow the sauce to simmer for a further 2–3 minutes or until it thickens. Serve immediately as a dip with Spring Rolls (see p.112). It will keep well in the fridge for up to 1 month.

Chinese Stock (Chinese-takeaway Style)

MAKES ABOUT 2 LITRES/3½ PINTS
3 or 4 chicken thighs (bone in)
3 or 4 pork spare ribs
½ small onion, sliced
2 spring onions, sliced
1 garlic clove, crushed
1 thumb-sized piece of ginger, sliced
1 teaspoon light soy sauce
1 teaspoon dark soy sauce
2 tablespoons Shaoxing rice wine

1   Put the chicken thighs, pork spare ribs, onion, spring onions, garlic, ginger, light soy sauce, dark soy sauce and 2.5 litres/4½ pints water in a large stockpot over a high heat.
2   Bring the pan to the boil and use a spoon to remove any foam that gathers on the surface of the liquid.
3   When the foam has stopped forming, reduce the heat to low and simmer the stock for 2–3 hours, then remove the chicken and pork pieces and strain the stock through a sieve into a fresh pan.
4   Add the Shaoxing rice wine and put the pan back on the heat. Simmer on low for a further 5 minutes, then set aside to cool completely. Transfer to a sterilised jar or airtight container and store in the fridge for up to 2 days. Or, freeze it in small quantities and defrost as needed.

Seasoned Oil (Chinese-takeaway style)

Use this fragrant, flavoursome oil to finish any Chinese stir-fry dish to great effect.

MAKES ABOUT 1 LITRE/35FL OZ
1 litre/35fl oz vegetable oil
2–3 star anise
½ cinnamon stick
1 small red onion, sliced
1 small brown onion, sliced
1 spring onion, halved
1 garlic bulb, peeled and roughly chopped
1 thumb-sized piece of ginger, sliced

1 Put the oil in a large saucepan and heat to 170°C/325°F. Carefully and slowly, add all the remaining ingredients to the oil and deep-fry for 7–8 minutes or until everything has turned a dark colour.

2 Use a slotted spoon to remove the vegetables and spices from the hot oil. Allow the flavoured oil to cool in the pan. When it's completely cool, transfer to a suitable container. Store in the fridge for up to 4 weeks, but allow it to sit at room temperature for 20 minutes before each use.

PART 4

Indian

British Indian curry is a cuisine all of its own and is perhaps some of the best proof possible of the positive things that can come out of the meeting of two cultures and peoples. Unlike traditional Indian food, British Indian, and indeed Scottish Indian, curry is a much more sauce- and gravy-filled affair, with spice and heat ramped up to spectacular levels at times!

Scottish curry culture is often inspired as much by Pakistani chefs as by Indian chefs, so the flavour and finish of particular dishes varies again, even from its counterpart dishes just a relatively few miles south in, say, Manchester or London. It's to Scotland and its curry culture that these revised recipes owe their origins and I very much hope you'll enjoy experimenting with them.

Rich, sweet and toffee-like, the Curry Broth is almost a complete curry, ready to be finished with just a few last-minute additions in order to make each sauce bespoke. It's one broth, simmering away gently, ready to be turned into korma, patia, south Indian garlic or tikka masala within minutes.

While the specific finish of the curry sauces themselves may differ slightly from region to region, curry fans from up and down the country are agreed on the required side dishes: poppadoms, spiced onions, vegetable and chicken pakoras, crispy naan and puri breads, fluffy basmati rice and much more besides.

Store-cupboard ingredients useful to have in stock in order to cook your favourite Indian takeaway food include:

Cumin seeds
Coriander seeds
Chilli powder

Garam masala

Turmeric

Dried fenugreek leaves (also known as methi)

Creamed coconut

Vegetable oil

Gram (chickpea or besan) flour

Fresh coriander

Tomato purée

Garlic & Ginger Paste (see p.217)

Aloo Tikki (Indian-restaurant Style)

These spiced potato patties are an excellent starter before any curry dish.

SERVES 1–2 (MAKES 4)

3 potatoes
1 green finger chilli pepper, chopped
Pinch of turmeric
Pinch of chilli powder
Pinch of ground cumin
Pinch of garam masala
Pinch of garlic powder
Pinch of ground ginger
¼ teaspoon sea salt
1 small handful coriander, chopped
1 egg, beaten
6 tablespoons breadcrumbs
Vegetable oil, for deep frying

1 Cut each potato into 2 pieces and add to a large pan of sea salted water. Boil the potatoes for 15 minutes or until soft. Drain the potatoes and return to the pan.

2 Add the chilli pepper, turmeric, chilli powder, cumin, garam masala, garlic powder, ginger and sea salt to the pan, then mash the potato mixture thoroughly. Add the chopped coriander and mix again.

3 Allow the mixture to cool slightly, then form into 4 round equally sized patties.

4 Put the beaten egg into a small bowl and spread out the breadcrumbs on a plate. Carefully dip the potato patties first into the egg mixture, then into the breadcrumbs.

5 Place the breaded patties on a plate, cover and refrigerate for at least 2 hours, or ideally overnight. This will help the coating stick to the patties when fried.

6 When you're ready to cook the patties, set your deep fryer to 180°C/350°F. Alternatively, fill a wok or large frying pan one third full with vegetable oil and heat to 180°C/350°F. The oil is ready when a few breadcrumbs dropped into the oil sizzle immediately. Place the aloo tikki patties carefully into the hot oil ad fry for 3–4 minutes, turning occasionally, until crisp and golden all over. Remove the patties from the oil using a slotted spoon, then drain off any excess oil on kitchen paper and serve the aloo tikki with Onion Salad (see p.96).

Baby Vegetable Pakora
(Indian-restaurant Style)

SERVES 2–3

3 onions, finely chopped, plus extra slices, to serve
2 small potatoes, finely chopped
1 large handful spinach leaves, finely chopped
1 small handful coriander, finely chopped, plus extra to serve
1 tablespoon dried fenugreek leaves
1 heaped tablespoon cumin seeds
1 tablespoon coriander seeds
1 teaspoon chilli powder
2 teaspoons garam masala
¼ teaspoon turmeric
1 heaped teaspoon sea salt
2 heaped tablespoons Garlic & Ginger Paste (see p.217)
1 tablespoon tomato ketchup
1 heaped teaspoon natural yogurt
Around 15 tablespoons gram (chickpea) flour
Vegetable oil, for deep frying
Lemon wedges, to serve

1 In a large bowl, combine the onions, potatoes, spinach leaves and
   coriander. Mix well.
2 Add the dried fenugreek leaves, cumin seeds, coriander seeds, chilli
   powder, garam masala, turmeric, sea salt and garlic & ginger paste.
   Mix thoroughly and set aside for around 1 hour. (During this time,
   the sea salt will encourage the onions to leach water and the
   mixture will become wet. This avoids the need to add too much
   water to the mix and delivers a superior final flavour.)
3 After 1 hour, add the tomato ketchup and natural yogurt. Mix well
   again.
4 When you're ready to fry, add the gram flour a little at a time, mixing
   thoroughly between each addition and adding up to 2 tablespoons

of water to achieve the right consistency. The amount of water the onions release will vary, meaning that you'll need to judge whether or not you need to add more water with the flour – take your time: the final mixture should be thick and sticky. Adding the flour only when you're ready to fry will help to ensure that you don't end up with thick and stodgy pakora.

5 When you're ready to cook the pakora, set your deep fryer to 180°C/350°F. Alternatively, fill a wok or large frying pan one third full with vegetable oil and heat to 180°C/350°F. The oil is ready when a few breadcrumbs dropped into the oil sizzle immediately. Use your hands to carefully form rough handfuls of the pakora mixture, then use two teaspoons to drop 1 teaspoon of the mixture into the oil at a time.

6 Fry the pakora for around 4–5 minutes or until cooked through, golden and crispy. (You will probably need to do this in batches.) Remove the cooked pakoras from the pan using a slotted spoon, drain off any excess oil on kitchen paper and arrange the pakoras on a plate. Decorate with finely sliced onion, coriander leaves and lemon wedges and serve with Pakora Sauce (see p.178).

Chicken Pakora (Indian-restaurant Style)

These are mildly spiced chicken pieces coated in a crispy gram-flour batter.

SERVES 2–3

2 large skinless, boneless chicken breast fillets (about 115g/4oz weight each)

1 teaspoon vegetable oil

1 teaspoon Garlic & Ginger Paste (see p.217)

2 teaspoons tomato purée

2 teaspoons lemon juice

125g/4oz gram (chickpea) flour

1 tablespoon dried fenugreek leaves

1 large handful coriander leaves, chopped

2 teaspoons ground cumin

½ teaspoon chilli powder

Vegetable oil, for deep frying

Thinly sliced onion and lemon slices, to decorate

Sea salt

1 Trim any excess fat from the chicken breasts and cut the meat into bite-sized pieces. Put the chicken in a bowl and add the vegetable oil, garlic & ginger paste, tomato purée and lemon juice and season with a pinch of sea salt. Mix well and set aside.

2 In a large bowl, combine the gram flour, dried fenugreek leaves, coriander, ground cumin, chilli powder and 1 teaspoon of sea salt. Mix well and add 120ml/4fl oz of water a little at a time until you have a smooth, thick batter. The consistency should be similar to that of double cream.

3 Add the chicken pieces to the bowl and allow them to rest in the batter for 20 minutes.

4 When you're ready to cook the chicken, set your deep fryer to 180°C/350°F. Alternatively, fill a wok or large frying pan one third

full with vegetable oil and heat to 180°C/350°F. The oil is ready when a few breadcrumbs dropped into the oil sizzle immediately. Drop the coated chicken pieces into the hot oil. Cook the pakora in batches, making sure not to overcrowd the pan. Fry each batch for 5–6 minutes, turning occasionally, until the batter turns golden and the chicken is cooked through. Remove the chicken pakora pieces from the pan using a slotted spoon and drain off any excess oil on kitchen paper.

5   Arrange the pakora on a plate or serving tray and decorate with sliced onion and lemon slices. Serve with Pakora Sauce (see p.178).

Haggis Pakora (Indian-restaurant Style)

Scotland's influence on Indian takeaway food continues to grow, with haggis pakora now a firm favourite on most Indian menus.

SERVES 1–2

5 tablespoons gram (chickpea) flour
½ teaspoon sea salt
¼ teaspoon garam masala
¼ teaspoon ground coriander
¼ teaspoon ground cumin
Pinch of turmeric
Pinch of chilli powder
½ teaspoon dried fenugreek leaves
3 slices of haggis, each cut into 4
Vegetable oil, for deep frying

1   In a large bowl, combine the gram flour, sea salt, garam masala, ground coriander, cumin, turmeric, chilli powder and dried fenugreek leaves. Mix well.
2   Add 60–75ml/2–2½fl oz water a little at a time until you have a smooth, slightly thick batter. The consistency should be similar to that of double cream.
3   When you're ready to cook the haggis pakora, set your deep fryer to 180°C/350°F. Alternatively, fill a wok or large frying pan one third full with vegetable oil and heat to 180°C/350°F. The oil is ready when a few breadcrumbs dropped into the oil sizzle immediately. Dip each piece of haggis into the pakora batter and place carefully into the hot oil. Fry for around 3–4 minutes or until the batter is crisp and golden.
4   Remove the haggis pakora from the pan using a slotted spoon and drain off any excess oil on kitchen paper. Serve with Onion Salad (see p.96) and Chilli Kebab Sauce (p.98).

Pakora Sauce (Indian-restaurant Style)

SERVES 2

About 120ml/4fl oz natural yogurt
2 teaspoons mint sauce
4 tablespoons tomato ketchup
Pinch of chilli powder
½ teaspoon sugar
¼ teaspoon sea salt
Milk, to dilute

1 In a bowl, thoroughly combine the natural yogurt, mint sauce, tomato ketchup, chilli powder, sugar and sea salt.
2 Add a little milk, if necessary, until the sauce reaches the desired consistency.
3 Chill in the fridge for at least 30 minutes before serving with Baby Vegetable and/or Chicken Pakora (see pp.173 and 175 respectively).

Raita (Indian-restaurant Style)

This creamy dip will cool the palate, making it the perfect match to any spicy Indian curry.

SERVES 2

½ tomato, peeled, deseeded and finely chopped
¼ cucumber, peeled and seeds removed
1 spring onion, finely sliced
About 120ml/4fl oz natural yogurt
¼ teaspoon ground cumin
¼ teaspoon ground coriander
1 small handful of coriander, chopped
¼ teaspoon sea salt

1   Combine the tomato, cucumber and spring onion in a bowl. Add the natural yogurt, ground cumin, ground coriander and fresh coriander, then the sea salt, and mix well.
2   Refrigerate the raita for at least 2 hours before using. Serve with any Indian curry.

Spiced Onions & Poppadoms (Indian-restaurant Style)

SERVES 1–2

1 large Spanish onion, chopped

3–4 tablespoons tomato ketchup

1 teaspoon mint sauce

½ teaspoon chilli powder

½ teaspoon sea salt

Large pinch garam masala

1 small handful coriander, finely chopped (optional)

1 box ready-to-fry poppadoms

Vegetable oil, for deep frying

1　In a large bowl, combine the onion, tomato ketchup, mint sauce, chilli powder, sea salt, garam masala and coriander (if using). Mix thoroughly and set aside in the fridge for at least 1 hour.

2　When you're ready to cook the poppadoms, set your deep fryer to 180°C/350°F. Alternatively, fill a wok or large frying pan one third full with vegetable oil and heat to 180°C/350°F. The oil is ready when a few breadcrumbs dropped into the oil sizzle immediately. Lower one uncooked poppadom into the oil and use tongs to press it down under the oil. The poppadom will instantly puff up. After 2–3 seconds, remove the poppadom from the oil, drain off any excess oil and set aside on kitchen paper. Repeat the process with the remaining poppadoms.

3　Serve the poppadoms and spiced onions as a starter or side dish with any Indian meal.

Shore-E-Murgh Spicy Chicken Wings (Indian-restaurant Style)

SERVES 2–3

6 tablespoons natural yogurt
1 tablespoon lemon juice
2 teaspoons Garlic & Ginger Paste (see p.217)
4 teaspoons Patak's Tikka Masala curry paste
¼ teaspoon dried fenugreek leaves
½ teaspoon chilli powder
½ teaspoon garam masala
Pinch of paprika
Pinch of turmeric
1 teaspoon sea salt
500g/1lb 2oz chicken wings, trimmed and prepared

1 Combine all the ingredients except the chicken wings in a large food-safe bowl.
2 Add the chicken wings to the bowl and mix thoroughly until the wings are evenly coated. Seal the container and marinate the wings in the fridge for at least 4 hours or ideally overnight. Remove the wings from the fridge 20 minutes before you intend to cook them.
3 Preheat the oven to 200 °C/400°F/Gas Mark 6.
4 Remove the wings from the marinade and arrange them on a wire rack above a baking tray. Put the wings in the oven and bake for 40–45 minutes until cooked through. Serve with Onion Salad (see p.96).

Pre-cooked Curry Chicken Breast (Indian-restaurant Style)

Almost every Indian takeaway restaurant pre-cooks their chicken breast, creating succulent, bite-sized pieces ready for use in any curry. The cooked chicken will freeze well and has the added advantage of ensuring that you can create your curry dishes without the need to handle raw meat every time.

MAKES ENOUGH FOR 6–8 CURRIES

6–8 large skinless, boneless chicken breast fillets (about 115g/4oz weight each)
¼ teaspoon sea salt
1 tablespoon lemon juice or lemon dressing
1 tablespoon tomato purée
1 tablespoon Garlic & Ginger paste (see p.217)
½ teaspoon turmeric
¼ teaspoon chilli powder
1 tablespoon vegetable oil

1   Trim any excess fat from the chicken meat and cut each breast into 4–5 pieces. Put the chicken pieces into a bowl and all the ingredients except the vegetable oil. Use your hands to mix well, then set aside for 5 minutes. Add the vegetable oil and mix thoroughly again.

2   Cover the meat and marinate in the fridge for at least 4 hours, or overnight if possible.

3   Preheat the oven to 150°C/300°F/Gas Mark 2.

4   Remove the chicken pieces from the marinade and arrange them on a large baking tray. Bake for about 20–25 minutes, until the chicken is tender and just cooked through. Remove the chicken from the oven and set aside to cool. You can store the cooked chicken in the fridge for up to 2 days, or freeze them for up to 3 months. If you freeze them, defrost thoroughly before using.

Pre-cooked Lamb (Indian-restaurant Style)

MAKES ENOUGH LAMB FOR 2 CURRIES
4 tablespoons vegetable oil
300g/10½oz diced leg of lamb
½ small onion, roughly chopped
Pinch cumin seeds
Pinch coriander seeds
1 garlic clove, crushed
1 teaspoon tomato purée
Pinch of chilli powder
Pinch of dried fenugreek leaves
Pinch of garam masala
¼ teaspoon sea salt

1   Heat the vegetable oil in a large pan over a medium heat. Add the
    lamb and onion and stir-fry for 1 minute until the lamb begins to
    brown. Add remaining ingredients, mix well and cook for 1 minute.
2   Add about 500ml/17fl oz of water to the pan – just cover the lamb.
    Bring to the boil, reduce the heat to low, cover and simmer for about
    45 minutes, stirring occasionally, until the lamb is tender and
    cooked through.
3   Strain the lamb from the cooking stock and drain any excess liquid.
    Set aside to cool for use in Indian curry dishes. The cooked lamb
    pieces will keep well in a food-safe container in the fridge for 2
    days, or they can be frozen for up to 1 month.

Chicken or Lamb Tikka (Indian-restaurant Style)

This mildly spiced tikka marinade will create deliciously flavoured chunks of meat that will freeze well. Freeze in batches of 3–4 pieces each, to use in any of the curry dishes in this book.

SERVES 4

6 large skinless, boneless chicken breast fillets (about 115g/4oz each) or equivalent weight of boneless lamb leg steaks
1½ tablespoons tikka paste
½ tablespoon Garlic & Ginger Paste (see p.217)
4 tablespoons natural yogurt
2 tablespoons vegetable oil
2 tablespoons lemon juice
1 teaspoon mint sauce
1–2 drops of natural red food colour (optional)
½ teaspoon mild Madras curry powder
½ teaspoon ground coriander
¼ teaspoon ground cumin
½ teaspoon garam masala
½ teaspoon turmeric
¼ teaspoon chilli powder
¼ teaspoon cayenne pepper
1 teaspoon dried fenugreek leaves
½ teaspoon sea salt

1   Trim any excess fat from the meat and cut each chicken breast or lamb leg steak into 3–4 large pieces.
2   Combine all the other ingredients in a large bowl with 6 tablespoons of water. Mix thoroughly and add the meat, stirring it through the marinade to coat. Cover and marinate in the fridge for at least 4 hours or overnight if possible.

3 Preheat the oven to 200°C/400°F/Gas Mark 6.
4 Arrange the tikka pieces on a wire rack over a roasting tray and bake on the highest oven shelf for 7 minutes. Turn the tikka pieces and bake for a further 7 minutes. Turn the tikka pieces once more and bake for a further 5–6 minutes or until just beginning to char.
5 Serve the chicken or lamb tikka pieces as a kebab with Pitta Salad (see p.94), or cool and freeze for up to 3 months for use in Indian curry dishes.

Tandoori King Prawn (Indian-restaurant Style)

SERVES 1–2

120ml/4fl oz natural yogurt

1 tablespoon vegetable oil

1 teaspoon lemon juice

1 teaspoon Garlic & Ginger Paste (see p.217)

½ teaspoon sea salt

½ teaspoon ground cumin

½ teaspoon chilli powder

½ teaspoon garam masala

Pinch of turmeric

1 teaspoon dried fenugreek leaves

8–10 large raw king prawns

1 Combine all the ingredients except the prawns in a large bowl, mixing thoroughly.

2 Add the king prawns to the marinade and use your hands to mix gently. Set aside for 10 minutes.

3 Meanwhile, preheat the oven to 240°C/475°F/Gas Mark 9.

4 Wipe off any excess marinade from the prawns and arrange them on a baking tray. Place the tray in the oven on the highest shelf and bake for around 6–8 minutes or until the prawns are cooked. Serve the tandoori prawns with Onion Salad (see p.96) and Garlic Kebab Sauce (see p.99).

Curry Broth

This curry-base recipe is my best so far. Use it for all the curry recipes in the book for incredible results!

MAKES ENOUGH CURRY BROTH FOR 7–8 CURRIES.

2.5kg/5lb 5 oz large onions (peeled weight – about 15 of the largest
   onions you can find), peeled and quartered
1 salad tomato, quartered
2 garlic cloves
½ teaspoon cumin seeds
½ teaspoon coriander seeds
250ml/9fl oz vegetable oil
15g/½oz creamed coconut block
1 heaped tablespoon turmeric
1 teaspoon garam masala
½ teaspoon mild chilli powder
1½ tablespoons tomato purée
1 tablespoon sea salt

1 Put the onion pieces in a large stockpot. Add the salad tomato,
   garlic, cumin and coriander seeds, along with about 1.5 litres/52fl oz
   of water and bring to the boil. Cook over a medium–high heat for
   around 1½ hours.
2 Add the remaining ingredients, mix well, and cook for a further
   1 hour.
3 Take the pan off the heat and, using a hand blender, blend the
   ingredients until smooth. Return the pan to a low heat, cover and
   cook, stirring regularly, for a further 30–40 minutes or until the oil
   begins to separate. The broth will become thick at this stage and
   may spit a little, be careful.
4 Allow the broth to cool completely before portioning into
   200–250ml/7–9fl oz containers for future use in Indian curry
   dishes.

Traditional Curry Sauce (Indian-restaurant Style)

SERVES 1–2

½ teaspoon Garlic & Ginger Paste (see p.217)
½ teaspoon tomato purée
½ teaspoon chilli powder
Pinch of sea salt
1 small handful coriander, finely chopped
½ teaspoon dried fenugreek leaves
200–250ml/7–9fl oz Curry Broth (see p.187)
Cooked meat or vegetables (optional)

1   Put the garlic & ginger paste, tomato purée, chilli powder, sea salt, coriander and dried fenugreek leaves in a large wok or pan over a low heat.

2   Add 2 tablespoons of the curry broth and mix well. Increase the heat to medium and mix again before slowly adding around half of the remaining curry broth.

3   Add meat or vegetables (if using) and mix well. Allow the curry to simmer for a further 1 minute, then add the remaining curry broth. Mix once more and simmer for 2–3 minutes until the sauce is thick and piping hot. Serve with Naan Bread (see p.203) or Chapatis (p.205).

Patia Sauce (Indian-restaurant Style)

SERVES 1–2

½ teaspoon Garlic & Ginger Paste (see p.217)
½ teaspoon tomato purée
½ teaspoon chilli powder
Pinch of sea salt
1 small handful coriander, finely chopped
½ teaspoon dried fenugreek leaves
200–250ml/7–9oz Curry Broth (see p.187)
Cooked meat or vegetables (optional)
2 tablespoons tomato ketchup
1 teaspoon mango chutney
2 teaspoons lemon juice

1   Put the garlic & ginger paste, tomato purée, chilli powder, sea salt,
    coriander and dried fenugreek leaves in a large wok or pan over a
    low heat.
2   Add 2 tablespoons of the curry broth and mix well. Increase the
    heat to medium and mix again before slowly adding around half of
    the remaining curry broth.
3   Add the meat or vegetables, if using, and mix well again. Simmer
    the curry sauce for 1 minute, then add the remaining curry broth,
    then the tomato ketchup, mango chutney and lemon juice. Mix once
    more and simmer for 2–3 minutes until the sauce is thick and
    piping hot. Serve with Puri Bread (see p.211).

Madras Sauce (Indian-restaurant Style)

SERVES 1–2
½ teaspoon Garlic & Ginger Paste (see p.217)
1 teaspoon tomato purée
Pinch of sea salt
1 small handful coriander, finely chopped
1 teaspoon dried fenugreek leaves
200–250ml/7–9oz Curry Broth (see p.187)
2 teaspoons blended chilli in oil
Cooked meat or vegetables (optional)
1 teaspoon lemon juice

1   Put the garlic & ginger paste, tomato purée, sea salt, coriander and dried fenugreek leaves in a wok or large frying pan over a low heat.
2   Add 2 tablespoons of the curry broth and mix well. Add the chilli blend, increase the heat to medium and mix well before slowly adding around half of the remaining curry broth.
3   Add meat or vegetables, if using, and mix well. Simmer the curry sauce for a further 1 minute, then add the remaining curry broth. Add the lemon juice, mix once more and simmer for 2–3 minutes until the sauce is thick and piping hot. Serve with Puri Bread (see p.211).

Korma Sauce (Indian-restaurant Style)

SERVES 1–2

½ teaspoon tomato purée
200–250ml/7–9oz Curry Broth (see p.187)
Cooked meat or vegetables (optional)
1 heaped tablespoon white sugar
2–3 tablespoons coconut flour
150ml/5fl oz single cream, plus extra for serving

1   Put the tomato purée and 2–3 tablespoons of the curry broth in a
    wok or large frying pan over a low heat. Stir to combine, increase
    heat to medium and cook for 30 seconds, then add cooked meat or
    vegetables (if using).
2   Add the remaining curry broth and mix well. Slowly add the white
    sugar, coconut flour and single cream stirring between each addition
    to thoroughly combine. The mixture will thicken quickly but
    should loosen as you add the cream. If it seems too thick, add 2–3
    tablespoons of water to thin the sauce out a little.
3   Cook the sauce over a medium heat for 5–6 minutes or until just
    thick, stirring regularly.
4   Pour the cooked korma sauce into a serving dish and finish
    with a little extra single cream.

South Indian Garlic Sauce (Indian-restaurant Style)

SERVES 1–2

1 teaspoon vegetable oil
¼ red pepper, finely chopped
¼ green pepper, finely chopped
1 small onion, finely chopped
1 teaspoon Garlic & Ginger Paste (see p.217)
1 teaspoon tomato purée
¼ teaspoon chilli powder
Pinch of sea salt
1 small handful coriander, finely chopped
2 teaspoons dried fenugreek leaves
200–250ml/7–9fl oz Curry Broth (see p.187)
Cooked meat or vegetables (optional)
2 teaspoons blended chilli in oil
2 green finger chilli peppers, sliced
50ml/1½fl oz single cream
2 teaspoons ground almond
1 teaspoon butter
¼ teaspoon garlic powder
1 tablespoon lemon juice
Pinch of garam masala

1 Heat the vegetable oil in a wok or large frying pan over a low heat. Add the red pepper, green pepper and onion. Stir-fry for 2–3 minutes to soften a little, then add the garlic & ginger paste, tomato purée, chilli powder, sea salt, coriander and dried fenugreek leaves. Stir to combine.

2 Add 2 tablespoons of the curry broth and mix well. Increase the heat to medium, then slowly add about half of the remaining curry broth. Add the meat or vegetables (if using) and mix well.

3 Simmer the curry sauce for a further 2 minutes, then add the remaining curry broth, the blended chilli in oil, green chilli peppers, single cream, almond powder, butter and garlic powder. Mix well and cook for a further 2–3 minutes or until the sauce becomes rich and thick.

4 Finally, stir in the lemon juice and garam masala and serve with Naan Bread (see p.203) or Chapatis (p.205).

Chasni Sauce

SERVES 1–2

½ teaspoon Garlic & Ginger Paste (see p.217)
½ teaspoon tomato purée
½ teaspoon chilli powder
Pinch of sea salt
1 small handful coriander, finely chopped
½ teaspoon dried fenugreek leaves
200–250ml/7–9oz Curry Broth (see p.187)
Cooked meat or vegetables (optional)
1 teaspoon ground almonds (optional)
2 tablespoons tomato ketchup
1 teaspoon mint sauce
1 teaspoon mango chutney
2 teaspoons lemon juice
100ml/3½fl oz single cream
Pinch of garam masala

1 Put garlic & ginger paste, tomato purée, chilli powder, sea salt, coriander and dried fenugreek leaves in a wok or large frying pan over a low heat.

2 Add 2 tablespoons of the curry broth and mix well. Increase the heat to medium, stir again, then slowly add about half of the remaining curry broth.

3 Add meat or vegetables (if using) and ground almonds (if using) and mix well. Simmer the curry sauce for a further 2 minutes, then add the remaining curry broth, tomato ketchup, mint sauce, mango chutney and lemon juice. Mix once more and simmer for 2–3 minutes until the sauce begins to thicken.

4 Finally, add the single cream and garam masala and stir to combine. Simmer for a further 1–2 minutes and serve.

Tikka Masala Sauce

SERVES 1–2

½ teaspoon Garlic & Ginger Paste (see p.217)
½ teaspoon tomato purée
½ teaspoon chilli powder
Pinch of sea salt
1 small handful coriander, finely chopped
½ teaspoon dried fenugreek leaves
200–250ml/7–9oz Curry Broth (see p.187)
Cooked meat or vegetables (optional)
3–4 tablespoons tikka masala marinade (see p.184)
100ml/3½fl oz single cream
1 tablespoon coconut flour
2 teaspoons sugar

1   Put garlic & ginger paste, tomato purée, chilli powder, sea salt, coriander and dried fenugreek leaves in a wok or large frying pan over a low heat.
2   Add 2 tablespoons of the curry broth and mix well. Increase the heat to medium, stir again, then slowly add about half of the remaining curry broth.
3   Add the meat or vegetables (if using) and mix well. Simmer the sauce for a further 1 minute, then add the remaining curry broth, stir again, and simmer for 2–3 minutes.
4   Add the remaining ingredients, mix well, and simmer for a further 3–4 minutes, adding a touch of water to loosen the sauce, if necessary. Simmer until the sauce is well reduced and smooth and serve with Mushroom Fried Rice (see p.214).

Jalfrezi Sauce (Indian-restaurant Style)

SERVES 1–2

Vegetable oil, for stir frying

1 onion, sliced

½ red pepper, sliced

½ green pepper, sliced

½ teaspoon Garlic & Ginger Paste (see p.217)

½ teaspoon tomato purée

½ teaspoon chilli powder

Pinch of sea salt

1 small handful coriander, finely chopped

½ teaspoon dried fenugreek leaves

200–250ml/7–9fl oz Curry Broth (see p.187)

Cooked meat or vegetables (optional)

1 Heat a splash of oil in a pan over a medium heat. Add the sliced onion, red pepper and green pepper. Stir-fry for 3–4 minutes, then remove the softened vegetables to a plate and set aside to cool slightly.

2 Put the garlic & ginger paste, tomato purée, chilli powder, sea salt, coriander and dried fenugreek leaves in a wok or large frying pan over a low heat.

3 Add 2 tablespoons of the curry broth and mix well. Return the cooked onion and pepper to the pan, then increase the heat to medium and mix well before slowly adding about half of the remaining curry broth.

4 Add the meat or vegetables (if using) and mix well, then simmer the curry sauce for a further 1 minute, and add the remaining curry broth. Mix once more and simmer for 2–3 minutes until the sauce is thick and piping hot. Serve with Naan Bread (see p.203) or Chapatis (see p.205).

Mixed Vegetable Curry
(Indian-restaurant Style)

SERVES 1–2

1 large potato, peeled and cubed

2–3 large cauliflower florets, chopped

2 tablespoons frozen peas

½ teaspoon Garlic & Ginger Paste (see p.217)

½ teaspoon tomato purée

½ teaspoon chilli powder

Pinch of sea salt

1 small handful coriander, finely chopped

½ teaspoon dried fenugreek leaves

200–250ml/7–9fl oz Curry Broth (see p.187)

1 Boil the potato for around 10 minutes until just soft. Add the cauliflower florets and frozen peas and simmer for a further 2–3 minutes. Drain and allow to cool.

2 Put garlic & ginger paste, tomato purée, chilli powder, sea salt, coriander and dried fenugreek leaves in a wok or large frying pan over a low heat.

3 Add 2 tablespoons of the curry broth and mix well. Increase the heat to medium, stir, then slowly add about half of the remaining curry broth.

4 Add the cooked vegetables and mix well. Simmer the curry sauce for a further 1 minute, then add the remaining curry broth. Mix once more and simmer for 2–3 minutes until the sauce is thick and piping hot. Serve with Naan Bread (see p.203) or Chapatis (see p.205).

Tarka Dal (Indian-restaurant Style)

This basic dal is very nutritious and can be flavoured with any number of different spices or 'tarka'. Plain dal can be prepared in advance, reheated and finished with the tarka just before serving, making it an extremely convenient dish. It will freeze well for up to 1 month. You can store it in 5–6 tablespoon batches and use it for dansak-style Indian curry dishes.

SERVES 1–2

60g/2oz red lentils (uncooked weight)
½ onion, thinly sliced
½ teaspoon turmeric
¼ teaspoon sea salt
3 tablespoons vegetable oil
½ teaspoon mustard seeds
¼ teaspoon cumin seeds
2 whole dried chilli peppers
3–4 curry leaves
Pinch of chilli powder
2 teaspoons Garlic & Ginger Paste (see p.217)
1 tomato, finely chopped
1 small handful of coriander, chopped, plus extra to decorate

1   Put the lentils in a colander and wash under running water until the water runs clear.
2   Put the lentils, onion and turmeric in a pan with 500ml/ 18fl oz of water over a high heat. Bring to the boil, skimming off any froth that forms on the surface of the liquid.
3   When the froth has subsided, reduce the heat to low and simmer the lentils for 40–45 minutes until soft, stirring often to ensure the lentils don't catch on the bottom of the pan. Add more water if the pan looks dry.
4   When the lentils are soft, remove from the heat, add the sea salt,

then use a potato masher to mash the lentils a little. (At this stage, you can refrigerate or freeze the plain dal to use another time.)

5   To finish the tarka dal, heat the vegetable oil in a separate small pan over a medium heat. Add the mustard seeds, cumin seeds, dried chilli peppers, curry leaves, chilli powder and garlic & ginger paste. Stir-fry for 2–3 minutes, then tip the fried mixture into the cooked dal and mix well. Add the chopped tomato and coriander, mix well again and simmer on a low heat for 1–2 minutes.

6   Ladle the dal into a serving dish and decorate with a sprinkling of chopped coriander. Serve with turmeric rice and Chapatis (see p.205).

Chicken Biryani (Indian-restaurant Style)

SERVES 1–2

2 tablespoons vegetable oil

½ small onion, finely chopped

Pinch of sea salt

1 teaspoon dried fenugreek leaves

1 tablespoon almonds

1 tablespoon raisins

1 tablespoon sultanas

1 portion of Pre-cooked Curry Chicken (see p.182), shredded

2 teaspoons Madras curry powder

1 portion cooked and cooled basmati Boiled Rice (see p.156)

3–4 thin slices of tomato

3–4 cucumber slices

1 tablespoon finely chopped coriander

1 portion of Traditional Curry Sauce (see p.188)

1   Heat the vegetable oil in a wok or large frying pan over a medium heat. Add the chopped onion, sea salt, dried fenugreek, almonds, raisins, sultanas and pre-cooked chicken. Mix well and stir-fry for 2–3 minutes.

2   Add the Madras curry powder and stir-fry for 30–40 seconds, then add the rice and mix well. Stir-fry for 3–4 minutes more, or until the rice is hot.

3   Transfer the chicken biryani to a serving dish and top with slices of tomato and cucumber and chopped coriander. Serve with the curry sauce.

Chicken Puri (Indian-restaurant Style)

To turn this puri sweet and sour, add 1 tablespoon tomato ketchup, 1 teaspoon mango chutney and 1 teaspoon lemon juice to the simmering sauce.

SERVES 1

½ teaspoon Garlic & Ginger Paste (see p.217)
½ teaspoon tomato puree
½ teaspoon mild chilli powder
Pinch of sea salt
1 small handful coriander, finely chopped
½ teaspoon dried fenugreek leaves
100–150ml/3½–5fl oz Curry Broth (see p.187)
4–5 pieces Pre-cooked Curry Chicken (see p.182), roughly chopped

1   Put the garlic & ginger paste, tomato purée, chilli powder, sea salt, coriander and dried fenugreek leaves in a wok or large frying pan over a low heat.
2   Add 2 tablespoons of the curry broth and mix well. Increase the heat to medium, stir, then slowly add about half of the remaining curry broth. Add the pre-cooked curry chicken.
3   Simmer the curry sauce for a further 2 minutes, then add the remaining curry broth. Increase the heat to high, mix once more and simmer for 2–3 minutes. Serve with Puri Breads (see p.211) and Onion Salad (p.96).

Bombay Aloo (Indian-restaurant Style)

SERVES 1

4–5 small new baby potatoes

½ teaspoon Garlic & Ginger Paste (see p.217)

½ teaspoon tomato purée

½ teaspoon mild chilli powder

1 small handful coriander, finely chopped, plus extra to decorate

½ teaspoon dried fenugreek leaves

100–150ml/3½–5fl oz Curry Broth (see p.187)

1 salad tomato, sliced

¼ teaspoon sea salt

1 Fill a large pan with water and add a pinch of sea salt, then tip in the potatoes. Bring the water to the boil over a high heat.

2 Once the water is boiling, reduce the heat to medium and simmer for 7–8 minutes, until the potatoes are just soft. Drain the potatoes and set aside to cool, then slice each potato into 2 pieces. (You can cook in bulk and freeze the potatoes at this point, if you wish.)

3 Put the garlic & ginger paste, tomato purée, chilli powder, sea salt, coriander and dried fenugreek leaves in a wok or large saucepan over a low heat.

4 Add 2 tablespoons of the curry broth and mix well. Increase the heat to medium, stir, then slowly add around half of the remaining curry broth with the tomato.

5 Simmer the curry sauce for a further 1 minute, then add the remaining broth. Increase the heat to high, mix once more and simmer for 2–3 minutes.

6 Decorate the bombay aloo with more fresh coriander and serve with any Indian meal.

Naan Bread (Indian-restaurant Style)

This delicious Indian bread is the perfect accompaniment to any curry dish. The bread is traditionally cooked in a tandoor oven, which provides spectacular results. With a little effort, this home-cooked version is a very close second. If you have a very hot grill, the naan breads may be placed under the grill to finish cooking as opposed to being turned in the frying pan.

MAKES 4

300g/10½oz strong white bread flour
1 x 7g sachet of fast-action dried yeast
5 tablespoons natural yogurt
1 tablespoon vegetable oil
125ml/4fl oz whole milk
1 teaspoon sea salt
2 tablespoons black onion seeds (optional)
1–2 tablespoons melted butter, to finish

1 In a large bowl, combine the bread flour and yeast. Mix well. Add the natural yogurt, vegetable oil and half the milk. Set aside for 5 minutes.
2 Add the sea salt and the black onion seeds (if using). Mix well and slowly add the remaining milk until you have a soft dough. On a lightly floured board, knead the dough for 3–4 minutes, adding more flour if necessary until the dough becomes smooth. Shape the dough into a ball.
3 Lightly oil the bowl and return the dough to the bowl. Cover with a wet cloth and leave to rise for around 1 hour or until doubled in size.
4 Knock the air out of the risen dough and divide into 4 equal pieces. Roll each piece of dough out into a large teardrop shape, no larger than your frying pan.

5   Heat a dry, heavy, cast-iron frying pan over a high heat until smoking. Put the rolled-out naan dough into the frying pan and cook for 30 seconds, then move the naan bread a little to ensure it does not stick to the pan and encourage even browning. Cook for a further 1 minute.

6   Flip the naan bread over and continue to cook on the other side for a further 1–2 minutes or until cooked through.

7   Remove the naan bread from the pan and arrange on a plate. If serving immediately, brush the cooked naan with melted butter. If the naan breads are being made ahead of time, leave them dry and butter them after reheating when ready to serve.

8   As each naan bread is cooked, stack it on top of the previous one and re-cover the stacked naans with foil. As the naan breads cool a little they will become soft and chewy.

Variations

GARLIC AND CORIANDER NAAN

Melt 2 tablespoons of butter in a bowl. Add 2 teaspoons of garlic powder. Brush the hot, cooked naan with the garlic butter and immediately garnish with chopped coriander leaves.

PESHWARI NAAN

Add 2 tablespoons of pistachio nuts, 2 tablespoons of desiccated coconut and 2 tablespoons of raisins to a blender. Blitz well. Add a tablespoon of the blended mixture to each piece of flattened dough. Roll out the dough carefully once again and cook as normal.

Chapati Breads (Indian-restaurant Style)

These are soft and light flatbreads, ideal for mopping up any curry dish.

MAKES 8

240g/8½oz chapati flour, plus extra for dusting
½ teaspoon sea salt
1 tablespoon vegetable oil
1 tablespoon melted butter

1 Combine the chapati flour and sea salt in a bowl. In a measuring jug, measure out 160ml/5½fl oz water and add it a little at a time, mixing well between each addition until the dough comes together.
2 Empty the dough onto a work surface dusted with flour. Make a well in the middle of the dough and add the oil, then knead for 2–3 minutes, working the oil into the dough, until smooth.
3 Return the dough to the bowl, cover with a damp cloth and set aside to rest for 2 hours.
4 Divide the dough into 8 pieces. Roll each piece of dough into a ball. On a floured surface, very carefully roll each ball out into 15–20cm/6–8-inch circles. Try not to press down with too much force when rolling the chapatis as the dough is very fragile; be gentle and take your time. Set each chapati aside on a plate between layers of foil or baking paper, as you go.
5 Heat a dry frying pan on a medium–high heat. Place one chapati into the pan and leave for 30–40 seconds. Flip the chapati over and cook for a further 20 seconds. Flip the chapati once more and cook for a further 30–40 seconds, applying gentle pressure to the chapati with a spatula. The chapati should begin to puff up and inflate. Turn the chapati for the final time and cook for a further 10–20 seconds. Remove the chapati from the pan. If serving immediately, brush the chapati with a little melted butter.

6 Repeat the process until all of the chapatis are cooked. You can serve the breads immediately, or cool them and store them for future use. Reheat chapatis in a hot, dry frying pan for 30–40 seconds on each side and brush with melted butter. Serve with Chicken Tikka (see p.184) or with any Indian curry dish.

Paratha Breads (Indian-restaurant Style)

Every Indian curry deserves to be mopped up with some delicious bread. This crisp, flaky bread fits the bill perfectly.

MAKES 4

250g/8oz chapati flour, plus extra for dusting
Pinch of baking powder
Large pinch of sea salt
2 tablespoons natural yogurt
3–4 tablespoons melted butter or ghee

1   In a bowl, combine the chapati flour, baking powder and sea salt. Mix well. Add the yogurt and mix well once again. In a measuring jug pour out about 120ml/4fl oz of water and add it a little at time to the flour mixture, until the dough comes together.

2   Empty the dough onto a flour-dusted work surface. Knead the dough for 2–3 minutes or until smooth. Return the dough to the bowl, cover with a damp cloth and set aside to rest for 30 minutes.

3   Divide the dough into 4 equal pieces. Roll each piece of dough into a ball. On a floured surface, carefully roll out the dough ball into a 15–20cm/6–8-inch circle.

4   Brush the rolled-out paratha bread with melted butter or ghee. Roll the bread up like a sausage and, using floured hands, form into a dough ball once again. Roll out the dough again into a 20cm/8-inch circle. This creates a layer of fat within the dough similar to that made when preparing pastry. Repeat for the other dough balls, layering each bread on a plate separated by foil or baking paper, as you go.

5   Heat a tava pan over a medium–high heat until just beginning to smoke. Lower the heat to medium–low and place a rolled-out paratha bread onto the pan. Cook the paratha bread for around 1 minute, turning every 10–15 seconds. Lower the heat a little and

brush both sides of the paratha bread with melted butter or ghee. Continue to cook for a further 2 minutes, again turning every 10–15 seconds and pressing down with a spatula until cooked.

6 Repeat the cooking process with the remaining breads and serve with any Indian curry dish.

Aloo Paratha Breads
(Indian-restaurant Style)

MAKES 4

1 large potato
Pinch of sea salt
Pinch of ground cumin
Pinch of chilli powder
1 tablespoon finely chopped coriander
½ teaspoon lemon juice or lemon dressing
4 prepared Paratha Bread dough pieces (see p.207)
Chapati flour, for dusting
3–4 tablespoons melted butter or ghee
Sea salt and freshly ground black pepper

1 Fill a large pot with water. Peel the potato and chop it into 2 large
   pieces. Add it to the pan with a pinch of sea salt, place the pan over a
   high heat and bring the water to the boil.
2 Boil the potato for 15–20 minutes or until soft. Drain the
   water and return the pan to the heat. Reduce the heat to low and
   add the ground cumin and the chilli powder, then season with a
   pinch each of sea salt and black pepper.
3 Mash the potato mixture thoroughly. Switch off the heat and
   add the chopped coriander and lemon juice or lemon dressing. Mix
   well once again, then set aside to cool. Taking one paratha dough
   piece, roll out the dough to form a 20cm/8-inch circle.
4 Take one quarter of the potato mixture and place it in the
   centre of the dough. Wrap the dough around the filling and twist so
   that the potato mixture is sealed within the dough. Dust the stuffed
   paratha bread with a little chapati flour and roll out once again.
   Repeat for the other dough balls, layering each bread on a plate
   separated by foil or baking paper, as you go.
5 Heat a tava pan over a medium–high heat until just beginning
   to smoke. Lower the heat to medium and place the rolled-out

paratha bread onto the pan. Cook the bread for around 1 minute, turning every 10–15 seconds. Lower the heat a little and brush both sides with melted butter or ghee. Continue to cook for a further 2 minutes, again turning every 10–15 seconds and pressing down with a spatula until cooked.

6 Repeat the cooking process with the remaining breads and serve with any Indian curry dish.

Puri Bread (Indian-restaurant Style)

This silky fried Indian bread is an important part of the hugely popular Chicken Puri (see p.201) starter dishes (and chickpea versions, too) and is also an excellent accompaniment to any Indian curry.

MAKES 4

75g/3oz plain white flour, plus extra for kneading if necessary
50g/2oz wholemeal bread flour
Pinch of sea salt
Pinch of baking powder
1 tablespoon semi-skimmed milk
Vegetable oil, for deep frying

1   Combine the plain flour, wholemeal flour, sea salt and baking powder in a large bowl. Mix well, then add the milk along with about 50ml/2fl oz of water incorporating the dry mixture into the wet ingredients with a fork until the dough comes together.

2   Empty the dough onto a floured surface and knead for 3–4 minutes until smooth. Add a little more flour while kneading if necessary, to prevent the dough from sticking. Form the dough into a ball and place in a bowl. Cover with a damp cloth and set aside for 5 minutes.

3   Divide the dough into 4 pieces. Flatten each dough ball into a circle. Use a rolling pin to roll out each piece of dough on a floured surface into a 15cm/6-inch round puri. Set each puri aside on a plate between layers of foil or baking paper.

4   When you're ready to cook the puri, set your deep fryer to 180°C/350°F. Alternatively, fill a wok or large frying pan one third full with vegetable oil and heat to 180°C/350°F. The oil is ready when a few breadcrumbs dropped into the oil sizzle immediately. Carefully place the rolled-out puri into the pan. Immediately press down gently with a spatula. The bread will puff up within seconds.

5   Let the bread fry for around 20–30 seconds, then carefully flip
    the bread over. Fry for a further 20–30 seconds and remove from
    the pan. As the puri breads are cooked, drain them on kitchen paper
    and then wrap in foil until ready for use. The breads can be served
    straightaway or stored for several hours at room temperature.
    Serve as part of Chicken Puri (see p.201) or with any Indian curry
    dish.

Turmeric Rice (Indian-restaurant Style)

You can scale up the portions of this rice, but always keep the ratio of rice to water the same: 200ml/7fl oz water per 100g/3½oz rice.

SERVES 1
100g/3½oz basmati rice (uncooked weight)
¼ teaspoon turmeric

1 Place the basmati rice in a large bowl and cover with plenty of cold water. Set the rice aside for 30–40 minutes, draining and re-covering the rice with fresh water 3 or 4 times during this time.
2 Place the rice in a colander and rinse one final time until the water runs clear, then transfer the rice to a pan. Cover with water (200ml/7fl oz water per 100g/3½oz rice), add the turmeric and bring the water to the boil over a high heat.
3 When the water reaches boiling point, cover with a lid, reduce the heat to the lowest setting and leave the rice to cook untouched for 14 minutes. Switch off the heat and allow the rice to stand for a further 10 minutes, then serve.

Indian Fried Rice (Indian-restaurant Style)

SERVES 1

2 teaspoons vegetable oil

½ small onion, finely chopped

¼ teaspoon Garlic & Ginger Paste (see p.217)

½ teaspoon dried fenugreek leaves

¼ teaspoon sea salt

½ teaspoon Madras curry powder

1 portion cooked and cooled basmati Boiled Rice (see p.156)

1 Heat a wok or large frying pan over a medium heat. Add the vegetable oil, onion, garlic & ginger paste, dried fenugreek leaves and sea salt. Stir-fry the ingredients for 1 minute.

2 Add the curry powder and basmati rice to the pan and mix well. Stir-fry for 3–4 minutes or until the rice is fully heated through. Serve with any Indian curry dish.

Variations

MUSHROOM RICE

Add 5–6 small button mushrooms, sliced, at the frying stage with the onion mixture.

MIXED VEGETABLE RICE

Add 4 tablespoons defrosted frozen mixed vegetables (broccoli, cauliflower, carrots, peas) at the frying stage with the onion mixture.

Pilau Rice (Indian-restaurant Style)

SERVES 1

1 tablespoon vegetable oil
1 small onion, finely chopped
1 tomato, halved and thinly sliced
1 garlic clove, finely chopped or crushed
1 cinnamon stick
2 bay leaves
4 cloves
1 teaspoon ground coriander
Pinch of ground ginger
Pinch of sea salt
¼ teaspoon black pepper
1 portion cooked and cooled basmati Boiled Rice (see p.156)

1   Heat the vegetable oil in a wok or large frying pan over a
    medium heat. Add all the remaining ingredients except the rice and
    stir to combine, then add the basmati rice and stir again.
2   Stir-fry the ingredients for 3–4 minutes, finishing over a high heat
    until the rice is piping hot and fully reheated. Serve with any Indian
    curry dish.

Lassi (Indian-restaurant Style)

Reaching for a pint of water is a common mistake among rookie curry fans. Doing so is more likely to clean the taste buds, resulting in them being evermore alert to the heat from the spices! A yogurt- or milk-based drink is far more effective at taking the heat out, and this recipe will provide the perfect partner to any spicy curry.

SERVES 1
100ml/3½fl oz natural yogurt
200ml/7fl oz ice-cold water
Pinch of sea salt
2 teaspoons caster sugar
Seeds of 1 green cardamom pod
1–2 sprigs of mint, to decorate

1   Put all the ingredients except the mint in a blender and blitz until the mixture becomes frothy on top.
2   Pour the mixture into a glass or serving jug and decorate with the sprigs of mint.
3   Serve as a drink with with any Indian curry.

Garlic & Ginger Paste
(Indian-restaurant Style)

It's possible to scale down this recipe and make a smaller amount; however, your blender will cope better with a larger quantity of oil and so it's useful to make a large batch at one time. The paste will freeze well in small quantities (perhaps in ice-cube trays) for future use in curry dishes.

5 garlic bulbs, cloves separated
Piece of ginger equal to the amount of garlic, peeled and roughly chopped to fit in a blender
50–100ml/1½–3½fl oz vegetable oil

1   Put the garlic cloves in a bowl and cover them with another bowl, rim to rim to form an orb. Shake furiously for about 1 minute and the garlic cloves should mostly be peeled.
2   Remove the remaining garlic peel and place the cloves in a blender. Add the ginger and the vegetable oil.
3   Blitz the ingredients into a smooth paste, adding just a touch of water if necessary to ensure the mix becomes smooth.
4   Transfer the garlic & ginger paste into a sealable container and store in the fridge for 1–2 weeks or freeze, in batches for future use.

Blended Green Chilli (Indian-restaurant Style)

Add just a drop of this fiery chilli pureé will put a kick in any curry dish and is often preferred to chilli powder which can leave a raw, bitter taste.

20–30 green finger chilli peppers
1 garlic clove (optional)
100ml/3½fl oz vegetable oil

1   Remove the stems from the chilli peppers, roughly chop them and place them in a blender.
2   Add the garlic (if using) and the vegetable oil, and blitz until smooth. Transfer the blended chilli to a food container and store in the fridge, or freeze in small portions, for future use in curry dishes.

Seasoned Oil (Indian-restaurant Style)

Not a recipe, as such, but useful tips nonetheless! When Indian restaurant chefs cook their curry dishes, they frequently do so using 'seasoned oil'. Put simply, this is oil that has already picked up flavours and aromatics from previous use in cooking spicy pakoras. As such, it's easy to replicate at home.

After frying a batch of Baby Vegetable Pakora (see p.173), use a slotted spoon to remove the pakoras from the hot oil. Set the oil aside to cool in the pan, then once it's completely cool, transfer it to a suitable container. Use this oil in your next batch of Curry Broth (see p.187) for extra flavour.

Another way to obtain seasoned oil is to reclaim the separated red, spicy oil from the Curry Broth after it has cooked. This deep-red oil has a big flavour that you can use to great effect in cooking Indian fried rice dishes and so on.

If you don't like too much oil in your curry dishes, cook your Curry Broth with the required amount regardless and spoon off excess after cooking. This allows the oil to cook the spices in the Curry Broth properly, while still allowing you to remove excess oil and re-use it later to spice up stir-fry and rice dishes.

PART 5

Pizza & Chip Shop

Debate rages on as to who first invented and popular-
ised Fish 'n' Chips in Britain. But, there's no denying
that Italian immigrants in the early 1900s capital-
ised on the popularity of the dish and made it their
own. By the 1920s, Italian-owned chip shops existed
all around Scotland and, to this day, most towns and
cities of reasonable size in Scotland and beyond
remain home to at least one Italian-owned 'chippy'.

Oven-baked pizzas, cooked with a thin-crust and limited toppings, are authentically Italian, served alongside garlic bread and spaghetti for a taste of Italy at home. For the more indulgent, Pizza & Chip shops may offer a deep-fried, beer-battered pizza (Pizza Crunch) alongside the classic cod or haddock and chips. Desserts don't escape a battering either: you have to try the deep-fried Mars Bar at least once!

Of course, you can't visit a chip shop without having some chip-shop chips and, for the complete Scottish chippy experience, some chippy sauce! In the east of Scotland, customers will demand salt 'n' sauce; those from the west will always choose salt 'n' vinegar. You, of course, may choose either, or indeed both!

Thin-crust Pizza Base (Italian-restaurant Style)

MAKES 2

230g/8oz strong white bread flour
1 x 7g sachet fast-action dried yeast
1 teaspoon sugar
½ teaspoon sea salt
1 tablespoon olive oil

1   In a large bowl, combine the bread flour, dried yeast and sugar.
    Mix well. Add the sea salt and mix again.
2   Add the olive oil to the bowl and slowly add about 120ml/4fl oz of
    water until the dough comes together.
3   Flour a work surface and tip out the dough. Knead thoroughly
    for 3–4 minutes, until the dough becomes smooth. Then, shape the
    dough into a ball.
4   Rub the bowl with a little olive oil. Return the dough to the
    bowl and cover with a wet cloth or oiled cling film. Set aside for
    about 1 hour until doubled in size.
5   Knock the air out of the risen dough, divide it into 2 pieces and
    knead each piece for a further 1 minute. Reshape each piece into a
    ball again. You can either roll out the dough balls now to make 2
    pizzas, or freeze the balls as they are for up to 1 month.

Italian Pizza Sauce
(Italian-restaurant Style)

Try making this sauce with fresh basil, if it's available, rather than dried.

MAKES ENOUGH FOR 2–3 X 25CM/10-INCH PIZZAS
2 tablespoons olive oil
1 garlic clove, sliced
1 x 400g tin of plum tomatoes
2 teaspoons dried basil or dried Italian herbs
1 teaspoon sugar
¼ teaspoon sea salt
Pinch of black pepper

1   Heat the olive oil in a small saucepan or frying pan over a low heat, add the garlic and stir-fry for 1 minute, then add all the remaining ingredients.
2   Increase the heat and bring the pan to boiling point. Reduce the heat to low and simmer 15–20 minutes. Remove the sauce from the heat and set aside to cool for a few minutes.
3   Using a hand blender, process the sauce until it becomes completely smooth (alternatively, transfer the sauce to a blender or food processor and blitz until smooth). Allow to cool completely and store in the fridge for up to 3 days, or freeze for up to 1 month.

Sweet Pizza Sauce (Italian-restaurant Style)

This recipe makes use of some very basic ingredients to create a sauce with just a little sweetness, similar to that used in some of the world's most famous pizza-delivery restaurants.

MAKES ENOUGH FOR 2 X 25CM/10-INCH PIZZA BASES
250ml/9fl oz tomato passata
½ teaspoon vegetable oil
½ teaspoon sea salt
½ teaspoon white sugar
½ teaspoon garlic powder
½ teaspoon dried oregano
½ teaspoon dried Italian herbs

1 Put all the ingredients in a small pan and stir well to combine.
2 Place the pan over a low heat and simmer for 5–6 minutes or until the sauce becomes thick. Remove from the heat. Cool completely, transfer to an airtight container and store in the fridge for up to 3 days, or freeze for up to 1 month.

Instant Pizza Sauce
(Italian-restaurant Style)

MAKES ENOUGH FOR 1 X 25CM/10-INCH PIZZA
3 tablespoons tomato purée
1 tablespoon olive oil
¼ teaspoon garlic powder
Pinch of onion powder
1 teaspoon dried Italian herbs
Pinch of cayenne pepper
¼ teaspoon sea salt
Pinch of black pepper

1   Combine all the ingredients in a bowl.
2   Add 5–6 tablespoons of water, a little at a time, mixing
      thoroughly between each addition until the sauce reaches the
      desired consistency. Allow the sauce to rest at room temperature
      for 10 minutes before using.

Margherita Pizza (Italian-restaurant Style)

This is the classic pizza, topped simply with sauce, mozzarella cheese and fresh tomato slices.

SERVES 1–2
1 ball of Thin-crust Pizza Base (see p.223)
2–3 tablespoons Sweet Pizza Sauce (see p.225)
100g/3½oz grated mozzarella cheese
2–3 slices fresh mozzarella cheese (optional)
1 salad tomato, halved and sliced
Pinch of dried oregano
Sea salt and freshly ground black pepper

1   Preheat the oven to 220°C/425°F/Gas Mark 7.
2   To prepare the pizza base, roll out the dough on a floured surface using a rolling pin. Place it on a well-floured board, then transfer to a lightly oiled 25cm/10-inch pizza tray and press the dough to the edges of the tray.
3   Spread the sauce thinly over the pizza base and sprinkle over half the grated mozzarella cheese. Top with the fresh mozzarella slices (if using), then the sliced tomato and finish off with the remaining grated mozzarella cheese.
4   Put the pizza in the oven and bake for 8–10 minutes or until the base is crispy and the cheese is golden.
5   Remove the pizza from the oven and sprinkle with the dried oregano and a pinch each of sea salt and black pepper.

Texas-style Barbecue Pizza (American Fast-Food Style)

SERVES 1–2

1 ball of Thin-crust Pizza Base (see p.223)

1–2 tablespoons Sweet Pizza Sauce (see p.225)

1 tablespoon barbecue sauce

100g/3½oz grated mozzarella cheese

¼ green pepper, sliced

¼ red onion, sliced

7–8 pepperoni slices

Pinch of black pepper

Pinch of dried oregano

1   Preheat the oven to 220°C/425° F/Gas Mark 7.

2   To prepare the pizza base, roll out the dough on a floured surface using a rolling pin. Place it on a well-floured board, then transfer to a lightly oiled 25cm/10-inch pizza tray and press the dough to the edges of the tray.

3   In a small bowl, combine the sweet pizza sauce with the barbecue sauce. Spread the mixture thinly over the pizza base, then sprinkle over half the grated mozzarella cheese, the green pepper, the red onion, and then the remaining grated mozzarella cheese. Top with the pepperoni slices.

4   Put the pizza in the oven and bake for 8–10 minutes or until the base is crispy and the cheese is golden.

5   Remove the pizza from the oven and sprinkle with black pepper and dried oregano.

Spicy Chicken & Sweetcorn Pizza (Kebab-shop Style)

SERVES 1–2

1 ball of Thin-crust Pizza Base (see p.223)
1–2 tablespoons Sweet Pizza Sauce (see p.225)
100g/3½oz grated mozzarella cheese
1 portion cooked Chicken Tikka, shredded (see p.184)
1–2 green finger chilli peppers, sliced
1–2 tablespoons sweetcorn, tinned or defrosted from frozen
Pinch of black pepper
Pinch of dried oregano

1   Preheat the oven to 220°C/425°F/Gas Mark 7.
2   To prepare the pizza base, roll out the dough on a floured surface using a rolling pin. Place it on a well-floured board, then transfer to a lightly oiled 25cm/10-inch pizza tray and press the dough to the edges of the tray.
3   Spread the sauce thinly over the pizza base and sprinkle over half the grated mozzarella cheese. Add the cooked chicken tikka, green chillies and sweetcorn, and top with the remaining grated mozzarella cheese.
4   Put the pizza in the oven and bake for 8–10 minutes or until the base is crispy and the cheese is golden.
5   Remove the pizza from the oven and sprinkle with black pepper and dried oregano.

Vegetarian Stuffed-crust Pizza (American Fast-food Style)

SERVES 1–2

1 ball of Thin-crust Pizza Base (see p.223)
1 or 2 cheese strings
1–2 tablespoons Sweet Pizza Sauce (see p.225)
100g/3½oz grated mozzarella cheese
¼ green pepper, sliced
¼ red onion, sliced
1 tomato, halved and thinly sliced
1 button mushroom, halved and thinly sliced
1–2 tablespoons of sweetcorn (tinned or defrosted from frozen)
Pinch of black pepper
Pinch of dried oregano

1 Preheat the oven to 220°C/425°F/Gas Mark 7.
2 To prepare the pizza base, roll out the dough on a floured surface, using a rolling pin. Place it on a well-floured board, then transfer to a lightly oiled 25cm/10-inch pizza tray and press the dough to the edges of the tray. Pull the cheese string(s) into pieces and arrange around the crust. Carefully fold the crust over the cheese string pieces and press down to seal in the cheese.
3 Spread the sauce thinly over the pizza base and sprinkle over half the grated mozzarella cheese. Add the green pepper, red onion, tomato, mushroom and sweetcorn, and top with the remaining grated mozzarella cheese.
4 Put the pizza in the oven and bake for 8–10 minutes or until the base is crispy and the cheese is golden.
5 Remove the pizza from the oven and sprinkle with black pepper and dried oregano.

Veggie Volcano (Kebab-shop Style)

SERVES 1–2

1 ball of Thin-crust Pizza Base (see p.223)
1–2 tablespoons Sweet Pizza Sauce (see p.225)
100g/3½oz grated mozzarella cheese
¼ green pepper, sliced
¼ red pepper, sliced
¼ red onion, sliced
2 green finger chilli peppers, sliced
Pinch of black pepper
Pinch of dried oregano

1. Preheat the oven to 220°C/425°F/Gas Mark 7.
2. To prepare the pizza base, roll out the dough on a floured surface using a rolling pin. Place it on a well-floured board, then transfer to a lightly oiled 25cm/10-inch pizza tray and press the dough to the edges of the tray.
3. Spread the sauce thinly over the pizza base and sprinkle over half the grated mozzarella cheese. Add the green pepper, red pepper, red onion and chilli peppers, and top with the remaining grated mozzarella cheese.
4. Put the pizza in the oven and bake for 8–10 minutes or until the base is crispy and the cheese is golden.
5. Remove the pizza from the oven and sprinkle with black pepper and dried oregano.

Garlic Pizza Bread
(American Fast-food Style)

SERVES 1–2

1 ball of Thin-crust Pizza Base (see p.223)
1 tablespoon butter, softened
1 teaspoon olive oil
1 teaspoon garlic powder
Pinch of dried parsley
2 tablespoons Sweet Pizza Sauce (see p.225)
100g/3½oz grated mozzarella cheese
Pinch of dried oregano
Sea salt and freshly ground black pepper

1   Preheat the oven to 220°C/425°F/Gas Mark 7.
2   To prepare the pizza base, roll out the dough on a floured surface
    using a rolling pin. Place it on a well-floured board, then transfer to
    a lightly oiled 25cm/10-inch pizza tray and press the dough to the
    edges of the tray.
3   In a small bowl, combine the softened butter, olive oil, garlic powder
    and dried parsley. Mix well.
4   Spread the pizza sauce thinly over the pizza base. Add the garlic
    butter and spread out as much as possible over the sauce. Top with
    the mozzarella cheese.
5   Put the garlic pizza bread in the oven and bake for 8–10 minutes or
    until the base is crispy and the cheese is golden.
6   Remove the pizza bread from the oven and sprinkle with a pinch
    each of sea salt, black pepper and dried oregano.

Oven-baked Garlic Bread (American Fast-food Style)

SERVES 1–2

2 tablespoons butter, softened
1 teaspoon garlic powder
¼ teaspoon onion powder (optional)
½ teaspoon dried Italian herbs or dried parsley
3–4 large slices of ciabatta bread
Sea salt and freshly ground black pepper

1   Preheat the oven to 220°C/425°F/Gas Mark 7.
2   In a bowl, combine the softened butter, garlic powder, onion powder (if using) and Italian herbs or parsley, along with a pinch each of sea salt and black pepper. Mix well.
3   Arrange the bread slices on a baking tray. Spread each slice generously with the garlic butter mixture.
4   Place the tray in the oven for 5–6 minutes or until the bread is crispy and golden.
5   Remove from the oven, leave to rest for 2–3 minutes and serve.

Breaded Mozzarella Cubes

SERVES 1–2
8 tablespoons plain flour
6 tablespoons panko breadcrumbs
½ teaspoon dried Italian herbs
¼ teaspoon garlic powder
¼ teaspoon onion powder
Pinch of cayenne pepper
1 egg
50ml/2fl oz whole milk
125g/4oz mozzarella cheese, cut into 7 or 8 cubes
Vegetable oil, for deep frying
Sea salt and freshly ground black pepper

1   In a bowl, combine half the plain flour with the panko breadcrumbs,
    Italian herbs, garlic powder, onion powder and cayenne pepper, along
    with a pinch each of sea salt and black pepper. Mix well and set aside.
2   Season the remaining flour with a pinch each of sea salt and pepper
    and spread it over a plate. Put the egg and milk in a bowl and mix
    thoroughly to combine.
3   Keeping one hand dry, dip the cheese cubes first into the plain flour,
    then into the egg and milk mixture, and finally into the seasoned
    breadcrumbs.
4   When you're ready to cook the mozzarella, set your deep fryer to
    180°C/350°F. Alternatively, fill a wok or large frying pan one third
    full with vegetable oil and heat to 180°C/350°F. The oil is ready
    when a few breadcrumbs dropped into the oil sizzle immediately.
    Deep-fry the breaded cheese cubes for about 2–3 minutes or until
    the breadcrumbs begin to turn crisp and golden. Once cooked,
    remove the mozzarella cubes from the pan using a slotted spoon
    and drain off any excess oil on kitchen paper.
5   Arrange the breaded mozzarella cubes on a serving dish and serve
    with a selection of dips.

Spaghetti Bolognese
(Italian-restaurant Style)

The smooth meat and tomato sauce hides a wide variety of
healthy fruit and vegetables, ideal for encouraging healthy
eating in kids! Bolognese sauce freezes well and you can use it
to make lasagne or even Bolognese French-bread pizza!

SERVES 4

2 x 400g tins of chopped tomatoes
2 small onions, chopped
1 carrot, chopped
1 red pepper, chopped
1 green pepper, chopped
3 garlic cloves
2 apples, chopped
3–4 button mushrooms, halved
500g/1lb 2oz beef mince
1 tablespoon tomato purée
1 tablespoon Worcestershire sauce
1 tablespoon paprika
1 teaspoon sea salt
½ teaspoon black pepper
¼ teaspoon dried Italian herbs
¼ teaspoon dried parsley
300–400g/10½–14oz spaghetti (dry weight)
1 teaspoon salted butter
1 small handful of grated mild Cheddar cheese

1   Put the tinned chopped tomatoes, onions, carrot, red pepper, green
    pepper, garlic, apples and mushrooms in a large bowl and use a stick
    blender to blitz until completely smooth. (Alternatively, do this in
    batches in a food processor or blender.)

2 Put the mince in a large pan over a medium heat and brown the mince for 2–3 minutes, breaking and stirring the meat constantly. Once browned, drain off any excess fat and reduce the heat to low. Add the tomato purée and Worcestershire sauce and stir-fry gently for 3–4 minutes.

3 Add the prepared tomato-and-vegetable sauce and mix well. Add the paprika, sea salt, black pepper, Italian herbs and parsley. Mix well once again and simmer on a low heat for 1½ hours. If the sauce becomes too thick, add a little water during cooking.

4 Bring a large pan of water to the boil. Add the spaghetti and stir once. Allow the spaghetti to simmer over a medium–high heat for 5–6 minutes or until just cooked. Drain the spaghetti and mix well with 2–3 tablespoons of Bolognese sauce. Add the butter and the grated cheese and mix thoroughly. Serve with garlic bread.

Garlic Cream Fettucine with Bacon & Mushrooms (Italian-restaurant Style)

This pasta dish is full of indulgence, with cream, Parmesan cheese and bacon.

SERVES 1–2

1 teaspoon olive oil
4 slices of smoked bacon, cut into thin strips
3 large chestnut mushrooms, thinly sliced
1 large garlic clove, finely chopped
½ small onion, finely chopped
1 teaspoon butter
75ml/2½fl oz double cream
75ml/2½fl oz semi-skimmed milk mixed with ¼ teaspoon cornflour
1 tablespoon grated Parmesan cheese
100g/3½oz fettuccine pasta (uncooked weight)
Sea salt and freshly ground black pepper

1   Heat the oil in a large frying pan over a medium heat. Add the bacon and mushrooms and stir-fry for 6–7 minutes.
2   Add the garlic and onion. Stir-fry for a further 1 minute, then add the butter, double cream, semi-skimmed milk and Parmesan cheese. Season with a pinch each of sea salt and pepper, stir thoroughly, then cook for a further 3–4 minutes or until the sauce just starts to thicken.
3   Fill a large pan with water and bring to the boil. Add a pinch of sea salt and the fettuccine pasta. Stir once and simmer for 5–6 minutes or until the pasta is just cooked. Drain the pasta through a sieve, reserving a little of the cooking water. Add the pasta and remaining water to the frying pan and stir well until completely coated in the cream sauce. Serve with garlic bread.

Beer-battered Fish with Instant Mushy Peas (Chip-shop Style)

SERVES 1–2

6–7 tablespoons plain flour

2 tablespoons cornflour

2 pinches of bicarbonate of soda (baking soda)

2 tablespoons vegetable oil, plus extra for deep frying

350–400ml/12–14fl oz beer or lager

2 fillets of haddock, cod or lemon sole (each about 140g/5oz), patted dry with kitchen paper

Lemon wedges, to serve

Sea salt and freshly ground black pepper

FOR THE INSTANT MUSHY PEAS (SERVES 2):

250g/9oz frozen peas

1 large tablespoon of salted butter

1 small handful mint, roughly chopped

¼ teaspoon sea salt

Pinch of black pepper

1 First, make the mushy peas. Boil or steam the frozen peas according to the packet instructions, until tender. Drain, transfer to an ovenproof bowl and add the butter, mint, salt and pepper. Roughly mash, combining everything fully as you go, then set aside and keep warm.

2 In a large bowl, combine 4 tablespoons of the plain flour with the cornflour, bicarbonate of soda, vegetable oil and beer or lager, along with ½ teaspoon sea salt and a pinch of black pepper. Mix well to from a thin batter with the consistency of single cream.

3 Season the remaining flour with a pinch of sea salt and pepper and spread the mixture out on a plate.

4   When you're ready to cook the fish, set your deep fryer to 180°C/350°F. Alternatively, fill a wok or large frying pan one third full with vegetable oil and heat to 180°C/350°F. The oil is ready when a few breadcrumbs dropped into the oil sizzle immediately.

5   Dust the fish in the seasoned flour, shaking off any excess. Dip the fish into the batter, again allowing any excess to drip off. Carefully place the fish into the hot oil and fry for around 5 minutes. Turn the fish only once during frying. (Do this in batches, if necessary.)

6   When the fish is cooked and the batter is golden and crisp, remove from the oil. Drain off any excess oil on kitchen paper and place on a sheet of greaseproof paper. Season with sea salt and allow to stand for 1–2 minutes before serving with lemon wedges, mushy peas and Chip-shop Chips (see p.241).

Special Fish (Chip-shop Style)

SERVES 1

1 large haddock or cod fillets, patted dry
1 egg, beaten
4 tablespoons breadcrumbs
2 tablespoons vegetable oil
2 lemon slices, to decorate
Sea salt

1   Check the fish fillet for any small bones and remove them.
2   Put the beaten egg in a large bowl and spread the breadcrumbs out
    over a large plate, then set aside.
3   Keeping one hand dry, dip the fish fillet into the egg, then into
    the breadcrumbs. Press down gently so that the crumbs stick to the
    fish.
4   Heat the oil in a frying pan over a medium heat. Fry the breaded fish
    for 2–3 minutes per side or until cooked through and golden.
    Remove the fish from the pan, drain off any excess oil and decorate
    with lemon slices. Season to taste with sea salt and serve with
    Chip-shop Chips (see p.241) and Instant Mushy Peas (p.238).

Chip-shop Chips (Chip-shop Style)

Maris Piper or King Edward potatoes will produce by far the best results when making chips. The method in this recipe takes a little time but delivers good results and allows the home cook to prepare chips in advance and finish them off in batches when hungry guests are ready to eat.

SERVES 1

200–250g/7–9oz potatoes, peeled and sliced into 1cm/½-inch thick chips

Vegetable oil, for deep frying

Sea salt and vinegar, to serve

1 Wash the chips thoroughly in cold water for 1–2 minutes. Fill a large pan with water and bring to the boil. Add the chips and simmer for 3–4 minutes. Remove the chips from the water and drain thoroughly. Set aside to cool.

2 When you're ready to cook the chips, set your deep fryer to 180°C/350°F. Alternatively, fill a wok or large frying pan one third full with vegetable oil and heat to 180°C/350°F. The oil is ready when a few breadcrumbs dropped into the oil sizzle immediately. Add the chips in small batches and fry for a few minutes until the chips just begin to soften. Remove the chips from the pan before they begin to take on any colour, and drain excess oil from the chips. Set aside in the fridge until cold or until ready for use. Allow the oil to cool in the pan, and reserve.

3 When you're ready to cook the chips, reheat the vegetable oil as in step 2. Add the chips in batches once again and fry for 5–6 minutes more, or until the chips have turned golden and crisp. Remove them from the pan, drain off any excess oil and serve with sea salt and vinegar.

Potato Fritters (Chip-shop Style)

SERVES 2–3

4 heaped tablespoons plain flour
2 heaped tablespoons cornflour
2 pinches of bicarbonate of soda
2 tablespoons vegetable oil, plus extra for deep frying
350–400ml/12–14fl oz beer or lager
2 large Maris Piper or King Edward potatoes, peeled and sliced
Sea salt and freshly ground black pepper

1 Preheat the oven to 180°C/350°F/Gas Mark 4.
2 Combine 4 tablespoons of the plain flour with the cornflour, bicarbonate of soda, 2 tablespoons vegetable oil and beer or lager, along with ½ teaspoon sea salt and a pinch of black pepper. Mix well until you create a thin batter with the consistency of single cream.
3 Season the remaining flour with sea salt and pepper, then spread the seasoned flour out on a plate. Dry the potato slices with kitchen paper.
4 When you're ready to cook the fritters, set your deep fryer to 180°C/350°F. Alternatively, fill a wok or large frying pan one third full with vegetable oil and heat to 180°C/350°F. The oil is ready when a few breadcrumbs dropped into the oil sizzle immediately.
5 Dust the potato slices in the seasoned flour, shaking off any excess. Dip the slices into the batter and again allow any excess to drip off. Carefully place the potato slices into the hot oil and fry for about 3–4 minutes. Turn the fritters only once during frying.
6 When the fritters are cooked and the batter is golden and crisp, remove them from the oil. Drain off any excess oil on kitchen paper and place the fritters on a sheet of greaseproof paper.
7 Place the fritters on a baking tray and put in the oven for 5–6 minutes, then remove from the oven, season with sea salt and allow to stand for 1–2 minutes before serving with a crispy roll and extra sea salt and vinegar on the side.

King Rib (Chip-shop Style)

SERVES 1
About 115g/4oz pork mince
Pinch of sugar
Vegetable oil, for frying
2 tablespoons barbecue sauce
120g/4oz plain flour
60g/2oz cornflour
Pinch of bicarbonate of soda
1 teaspoon sea salt
About 200ml/7fl oz beer
Sea salt and freshly ground black pepper

1   In a large bowl, combine the mince and sugar with a generous pinch each of sea salt and black pepper. Mix well and roll the mince into a ball.

2   Lay the mince ball on a sheet of greaseproof paper and place another sheet on top. Flatten the mince into a thin oval-shaped patty. Cover and freeze for at least 2 hours.

3   Heat a little oil in a pan over a low–medium heat. Place the frozen pork patty into the pan and fry for 4 minutes, turning occasionally.

4   Baste the patty on both sides with the barbecue sauce, turning for a further 1–2 minutes so that the sauce cooks into the patty. Remove the pork from the pan and set aside to cool.

5   Once cooled, place the patty in the fridge for at least 1 hour to help the remaining sauce set onto the patty. (You can prepare the king rib up to this stage and leave it overnight to finish off the following day, if you prefer.)

6   In a large bowl, combine the plain flour, cornflour, bicarbonate of soda and sea salt. Mix well. Add the beer and whisk thoroughly until you have a smooth batter the consistency of single cream.

7   When you're ready to cook the king rib, set your deep fryer to 180°C/350°F. Alternatively, fill a wok or large frying pan one third

full with vegetable oil and heat to 180°C/350°F. The oil is ready when a few breadcrumbs dropped into the oil sizzle immediately.

8 Dip the pork quickly into the batter and drop carefully into the hot oil. Fry for 2–3 minutes or until golden, turning once or twice. Remove the king rib from the pan using a slotted spoon, drain off any excess oil on kitchen paper and season liberally with sea salt. Serve with Chip-shop Chips (see p.241).

Pizza Crunch (Chip-shop Style)

If you've ever had a pizza or pizza crunch from your local chip shop, you'll know which supermarket pizzas to purchase in order to make your own: small, inexpensive, fresh pizzas with just a little tomato sauce and cheese that won't fall off. You'll find them easily in all major supermarkets. Hugely indulgent, with a crispy batter coating, this one is a Scottish classic!

SERVES 1–2
4 heaped tablespoons plain flour
2 heaped tablespoons cornflour
2 pinches of bicarbonate of soda
2 tablespoons vegetable oil, plus extra for deep frying
350–400ml/12–14fl oz beer or lager
1 small supermarket cheese & tomato pizza
Vinegar, to serve
Sea salt and freshly ground black pepper

1   In a large bowl, combine the plain flour, cornflour, bicarbonate of soda, vegetable oil and beer or lager, along with ½ teaspoon of sea salt and a pinch of black pepper. Mix well until you create a thin batter with the consistency of single cream.

2   When you're ready to cook the pizza crunch, set your deep fryer to 180°C/350°F. Alternatively, fill a wok or large frying pan one third full with vegetable oil and heat to 180°C/350°F. The oil is ready when a few breadcrumbs dropped into the oil sizzle immediately. Cut the pizza in half. Dip the pizza slices into the batter and allow any excess to drip off. Carefully place the pizza slices into the hot oil and fry for about 1–2 minutes. Turn the pizza slices only once during frying.

3   When the pizza crunch is cooked and the batter is golden and crisp, remove the slices from the oil. Drain off any excess oil on kitchen paper and place onto greaseproof paper. Season with a little sea salt and serve with Chip-shop Chips (see p.241) and extra sea salt and vinegar on the side.

Chippy Sauce (Chip-shop Style)

In the east of Scotland, 'sea salt 'n' sauce' is the preferred topping to any chip-shop dish. The thin, tangy brown sauce has become famous through the years and can often be found on chip-shop counters, poured into old Irn-Bru bottles.

MAKES ABOUT 200ML/7FL OZ

There is fierce debate on which watering-down method you should use to make the sauce. Many people argue that vinegar rather than water. Of course, vinegar costs money while tap water is free! Feel free to try both variations on the sauce and I hope you'll agree that water is the true necessary ingredient.

180ml/6fl oz bottle 'gold star' brown sauce
30ml/1fl oz water or vinegar

1   Mix the brown sauce and water or vinegar thoroughly.
2   Serve with chips or any chip-shop dish. The sauce will keep well in the fridge for several days.

PART 6

Other Popular Dishes

While classic takeaway favourites such as pizza, fish & chips, and curry will always be popular choices, we're fortunate to live in an ever-more connected world that brings us cuisines from around the globe, even in the form of takeaway. From Japanese katsu (deliciously crispy fried chicken) to the aromatic delights of Thai green curry, this chapter includes a selection of dishes from around the world, along with a few lunchtime deli favourites.

....

Part 5

Other Popular Dishes

Chicken Katsu Curry
with Japanese Sticky Rice
(Japanese-restaurant Style)

If time is short, good Chinese curry sauce mixes such as Yeung's or Maykway provide a quick alternative to the Japanese curry sauce served with this recipe and will deliver good results.

SERVES 1

1 large skinless, boneless chicken breast fillet (around 115g/4oz weight)
4 tablespoons plain flour
6 tablespoons panko breadcrumbs
1 egg, beaten
6 tablespoons vegetable oil
Sea salt and freshly ground black pepper

FOR THE JAPANESE STICKY RICE (SERVES 1–2):
125g/4oz sushi rice

1   First, make the Japanese Sticky Rice. Wash the rice in cold water and set aside for 5 minutes. Drain the rice and replace the water with fresh water, then leave for a further 10 minutes. Place the rice in a sieve and rinse through one final time.
2   Put the rice in a pan with a tight-fitting lid along with 160ml/5½fl oz of water. Bring the water to the boil over a high heat, with the lid off the pan. Once the water starts to boil, put the lid on the pan, reduce the heat to low and simmer for 12 minutes or until the liquid has been absorbed. Switch off the heat and set aside with the lid on for at least 15–20 minutes or until ready to serve.
3   Meanwhile, make the Chicken Katsu Curry. Trim any excess fat from the chicken breast. Wrap the chicken between a folded

layer of cling film and use a meat mallet to pound the fillet until flat and thin. Season the chicken with a pinch each of sea salt and pepper.

4 Arrange the plain flour and the panko breadcrumbs on two separate plates. Put the beaten egg in a bowl. Keeping one hand dry, dip the chicken piece first into the flour, then into the egg and finally into the panko breadcrumbs. Press the breadcrumbs down firmly so that the chicken piece is completely coated. Set aside on a plate.

5 Heat the oil in a wok or deep frying pan over a medium heat. Fry the breaded chicken for around 4 minutes, then flip the chicken piece over and fry on the other side for a further 3–4 minutes, until the chicken is cooked through and the breadcrumbs are golden.

6 Remove the breaded chicken from the pan and drain off any excess oil on kitchen paper. Cut the chicken into 4–6 slices and arrange the slices on a plate. Serve with the sticky rice, and Japanese curry sauce (see p.251).

Japanese Curry Sauce (Japanese-restaurant Style)

SERVES 1

4 teaspoons margarine
½ small onion, finely sliced
1 heaped teaspoon Garlic & Ginger Paste (see p.217)
1 tablespoon plain flour
1 tablespoon hot Madras curry powder
250ml/9fl oz chicken stock
Pinch of garam masala

1   Heat a non-stick pan over a low heat. Add half the margarine and all
    the onion and stir-fry for 3–4 minutes or until the onions turn
    golden brown. Add the garlic & ginger paste and stir-fry for a
    further 1 minute. Remove the mixture from the pan and set aside.
2   Add the remaining margarine to the pan. Add the plain flour and
    mix well until the mixture forms a paste and the flour is cooked out
    (this will take around one minute; you'll know it's done when the
    flour no longer smells raw and instead a slightly toasted aroma fills
    the air). Add the curry powder and mix well again. The pan will
    become very dry at this stage. Slowly add a third of the chicken
    stock, stirring continuously as you do so. Press down on the sauce
    with a spatula in order to prevent any lumps from forming.
3   Add another third of the chicken stock and mix well, then
    return the spiced onion mixture to the pan and add the remaining
    chicken stock. Stir and simmer on a low heat for 6–8 minutes or
    until the sauce is well reduced and thickened. Add the garam
    masala and simmer for a final 30 seconds. Serve the curry sauce
    over Chicken Katsu Curry (see p.249) or with rice or chips.

Yakitori Chicken
(Japanese-restaurant Style)

You'll need six wooden skewers for this recipe. Soak them in
water for 30 minutes before using them to prevent them
burning when you cook the chicken.

SERVES 1–2

6 tablespoons soy sauce

1 tablespoon sake

1 teaspoon mirin

1 tablespoon white sugar

2 large skinless, boneless chicken breast fillets (about 115g/4oz
    weight per breast)

1 teaspoon vegetable oil, plus extra for brushing

1 teaspoon cornflour

1 leek or 1 large spring onion, cut into small bite-sized pieces

1   In a small pan, combine the soy sauce, sake, mirin and white sugar.
    Place on a high heat and bring to the boil, then reduce the heat to
    low and stir for 3–4 minutes or until the sauce begins to foam and
    reduces. Remove from the heat and set aside to cool.

2   Trim any excess fat from the chicken breast and cut each
    breast into 5–6 thin strips. Add 2 teaspoons of the prepared sauce
    and the vegetable oil. Use your hands to mix the chicken through
    the marinade, then leave to marinate for 5 minutes. Then, add the
    cornflour and mix well again.

3   One by one, thread the chicken strips onto 4 of the skewers,
    piercing each chicken piece several times, weaving in and out. Each
    skewer should comfortably hold 2 or 3 strips of chicken. Spear the
    leek or spring onion pieces on the remaining two skewers.

4   Heat a griddle pan to a medium–high heat. Brush the chicken
    and vegetable skewers with a little vegetable oil and place them
    carefully onto the griddle pan. Reduce the heat to medium and cook

the skewers for 3–4 minutes per side, basting with the remaining sauce, until the chicken is cooked through and beginning to char and the vegetables are soft. (The skewers will also cook very well on a double-plated health grill.) Remove the cooked chicken skewers from the griddle and serve as a starter, or with Japanese Sticky Rice (see p.249) as a main meal.

Thai Green Curry (Thai-restaurant Style)

SERVES 1–2

1 large skinless, boneless chicken breast fillet (average weight 115g/4oz)

1 red onion

1 tablespoon Garlic & Ginger Paste (see p.217)

2 finger chilli peppers

1 stalk of lemongrass

½ teaspoon ground coriander

½ teaspoon ground cumin

½ teaspoon white pepper

1 teaspoon brown sugar

Pinch of sea salt

1 small handful of basil leaves

1 large handful of coriander leaves and stems

2 tablespoons lime juice

2 teaspoons fish sauce

4 tablespoons coconut milk

2 tablespoons vegetable oil

200ml/7fl oz chicken stock, or 200ml/7fl oz boiling water mixed with ½ chicken stock cube

2 kaffir lime leaves

200ml/7fl oz coconut milk

1   Trim any excess fat from the chicken breast fillet and cut into bite-sized pieces. Set aside.

2   Make a Thai curry paste. Put the red onion, garlic & ginger paste, chilli peppers, lemongrass, ground coriander, ground cumin, white pepper, brown sugar, sea salt, basil, coriander, lime juice, fish sauce and coconut milk in a blender and blitz until fully combined. Set aside.

3 Heat a wok or frying pan on a medium heat. Add the vegetable oil and blitzed curry paste, then stir-fry for 1 minute. Add the chicken pieces and turn in the pan until fully sealed.

4 Add the chicken stock to the pan and bring to the boil, then add the kaffir lime leaves. Increase the heat to medium–high and cook the sauce for 8–10 minutes, gradually adding the coconut milk until the sauce is slightly thickened and the chicken is just cooked through. Allow the curry to cool slightly, then serve with fragrant Thai rice.

Piri Piri Chicken (Portuguese Style)

This spicy chicken is excellent with Coleslaw (see p.40) or even served inside a burger bun with lettuce and mayonnaise.

SERVES 1

4 tablespoons vegetable oil
½ red pepper, diced
2 garlic cloves, crushed
1 tablespoon white wine vinegar
1–2 finger chilli peppers
½ teaspoon sea salt
1 teaspoon dried oregano
2 tablespoons lemon juice
1 large skinless, boneless chicken breast fillet (about 115g/4oz weight)

1 Heat the oil in a pan and add the red pepper. Fry over a low heat for 3–4 minutes or until the pepper begins to soften, then add the crushed garlic and fry for 1 minute.

2 Add the white wine vinegar, chilli peppers, sea salt and dried oregano. Switch off the heat and stir the mixture for 10 seconds, then add the lemon juice along with 2 tablespoons of water and allow the mixture to cool slightly.

3 Pour the mixture into a blender and blitz for 30 seconds or until smooth. Transfer the marinade to a bowl and allow to cool completely.

4 Meanwhile, trim any excess fat from the chicken. Using a meat mallet, pound the chicken breast between two sheets of cling film until thin. Once the marinade is cool, add the chicken to the bowl and mix well. Cover the bowl and place in the fridge for at least 1 hour, or up to 4 hours if possible.

5   Heat a griddle pan over a high heat. When the pan is smoking, reduce the heat to medium–low. Cook the chicken breast for about 2–3 minutes on each side or until cooked through and charred.

Chicken Fajita Wrap
(Deli-sandwich Style)

Spicy, succulent pan-fried chicken strips with onion and peppers, wrapped in a soft flour tortilla. The optional processed cheese slice is a modern-day US fast-food addition to this classic Mexican dish.

SERVES 1–2

1 tablespoon cornflour
¼ chicken stock cube, crumbled
½ teaspoon dried oregano
1 teaspoon chilli powder
½ teaspoon cayenne pepper
1 teaspoon paprika
¼ teaspoon garlic powder
½ teaspoon onion powder
¼ teaspoon ground cumin
1 teaspoon sugar
1 large skinless, boneless chicken breast fillet (about 115g/4oz weight)
2 tablespoons vegetable oil
½ green pepper, finely sliced
1 onion, finely sliced
2 tablespoons lime juice
1 slice of processed cheese, halved (optional)
2 large flour tortillas
Sea salt and freshly ground black pepper

1   First, make a fajita mix. Combine the cornflour, chicken stock cube, oregano, chilli powder, cayenne pepper, paprika, garlic powder, onion powder, ground cumin and sugar, along with ¼ teaspoon of sea salt and a pinch of black pepper in a small bowl. Mix thoroughly.

2   Trim any excess fat from the breast fillet and cut the meat into 5–6 long strips.

3   Heat the vegetable oil in a large frying pan over a medium–high heat. Add the sliced green pepper and onion and stir-fry for 3–4 minutes, then remove from the pan and set aside.

4   Add a little more vegetable oil to the pan if necessary, then add the chicken breast strips and stir-fry for 1–2 minutes. Add 1 tablespoon of the prepared fajita mix (or to taste) and mix well. Add the lime juice and 50ml/2fl oz of water, then return the green pepper and onion mixture to the pan.

5   Mix well and continue to stir-fry for a further 3–4 minutes or until the chicken is cooked through and the sauce begins to thicken.

6   Arrange one half-cheese slice (if using) on each flour tortilla. Add a generous amount of the chicken, green pepper and onions. Fold and roll the fajita wraps. Serve with Guacamole (see p.268), soured cream and Pico De Gallo (p.269).

Tuna Mayonnaise Sandwich (Deli-sandwich Style)

The lemon juice in this recipe does not come through strongly in the finished sandwich, but helps to add a fresh flavour and cut the strength of the tinned tuna. You could also stir tinned sweetcorn through the tuna mayonnaise, if you like, to give extra crunch to your sandwich. Alternatively, add thin slices of cucumber for a further burst of freshness.

SERVES 1

1 x 185g tin of tuna in spring water
3 tablespoons mayonnaise
2 teaspoons lemon juice
Pinch of sea salt
2 slices of granary or wholemeal bread

1   Drain the tuna and squeeze dry, then put it in a bowl with the the mayonnaise, lemon juice and sea salt. Mix thoroughly and set aside in the fridge for at least 1 hour or until well chilled.
2   Spread half of the tuna mayonnaise mixture onto one slice of bread, top with the remaining bread slice, divide the sandwich into triangles and serve. The remaining tuna mayo will keep well in the fridge for up to 2 days.

Coronation Chicken Sub (Deli-sandwich Style)

SERVES 1

1 large skinless, boneless chicken breast fillet (about 115g/4oz weight)

1 tablespoon olive oil

5–6 tablespoons mayonnaise

1 teaspoon mango chutney (optional)

1 teaspoon mild Madras curry powder

Pinch of chilli powder

1 tablespoon lemon juice

1 large sub roll or small French baguette

4 tomato slices

4 cucumber slices

1 handful of shredded lettuce

¼ red onion, finely chopped

Sea salt and freshly ground black pepper

1　Preheat the oven to 190°C/375°F/Gas Mark 5.

2　Place the chicken breast fillet onto a baking tray and drizzle with the olive oil, then season with a pinch each of sea salt and pepper. Cover loosely with foil and place on the middle shelf of the oven for 15 minutes, then remove the foil and bake for 10–15 minutes more. Remove the cooked chicken from the oven and set aside to cool.

3　In a small bowl, combine the mayonnaise, mango chutney (if using), curry powder, chilli powder and lemon juice.

4　When the cooked chicken breast is fully cooled, cut it into small pieces and put it in a large bowl. Add the prepared sauce and mix well. Refrigerate the coated chicken for at least 2 hours to allow the flavours to mingle.

5　Slice the sub roll or baguette and fill it with the coronation chicken. Add the tomato slices, cucumber slices and shredded lettuce. Sprinkle with the chopped red onion and serve.

Chargrilled Chicken Sandwich (Deli-sandwich Style)

SERVES 1

1 large skinless, boneless chicken breast fillet (about 115g/4oz weight)
1 tablespoon olive oil
1 tablespoon poppy seeds
2 tablespoons mayonnaise
½ teaspoon honey
½ teaspoon Dijon mustard
2 slices of granary or wholemeal bread
4 tomato slices
4 cucumber slices
1 handful of shredded lettuce
Sea salt and freshly ground black pepper

1   Preheat the oven to 190°C/375°F/Gas Mark 5.
2   Heat a griddle pan to a high heat. Brush the chicken breast fillet with olive oil, and season with a pinch each of sea salt and pepper.
3   Place the chicken fillet onto the hot griddle pan and cook for 2–3 minutes. Turn the chicken breast over and cook on the other side for a further 2–3 minutes. Lift the chicken breast off the griddle pan and place it on a baking tray. Place the tray on the middle shelf of the oven and bake for 15–20 minutes or until cooked through. Remove the cooked chicken from the oven and set aside to cool.
4   Heat a dry frying pan on a medium heat. Add the poppy seeds and toast in the pan for 1–2 minutes, stirring occasionally. Remove the seeds from the pan and set aside to cool.
5   In a small bowl, combine the mayonnaise, honey and Dijon mustard. Mix thoroughly. Spread the mixture generously on both slices of the bread, reserving a little.
6   Slice the chicken into strips and add to the sandwich. Add a

little extra honey mustard mayonnaise on top of the chicken pieces and sprinkle with the toasted poppy seeds. Add the tomato slices, cucumber slices and shredded lettuce. Top with the remaining bread slice, cut the sandwich into two triangles and serve.

Cheese & Onion Sandwich (Deli-sandwich Style)

SERVES 1

½ small onion, finely chopped

40g/1½oz grated Cheddar cheese

1–2 tablespoons mayonnaise

1 tablespoon finely chopped chives (optional)

2 slices of white bread

1 In a bowl, combine the onion, cheese and mayonnaise. Mix well, adding more mayonnaise if necessary, then add the chopped chives (if using) and stir again.

2 Spread one slice of bread generously with the prepared cheese-and-onion mixture. Add the remaining bread slice, cut the sandwich into two triangles and serve.

Tortilla Wraps

MAKES 10–12

360g/12½oz plain white flour, plus extra for dusting

¼ teaspoon sea salt

½ tablespoon baking powder

3 tablespoons vegetable oil

230ml/8fl oz warm water

1 In a large bowl, combine the plain flour, sea salt and baking powder. Mix well. Add the vegetable oil and mix once more.

2 Slowly add the water, stirring occasionally until a dough begins to form. Tip out the dough onto a flour-dusted surface and knead for 3–4 minutes until smooth. Add a little more flour while kneading if necessary to prevent the dough from sticking.

3 Divide the dough into 10–12 pieces. Roll each piece into a ball, place on a tray and and cover with a slightly damp cloth. Leave to rest for 30 minutes.

4 Flatten each dough ball into a circle, then use a rolling pin to roll out each one into a 20–25cm/8–10-inch round tortilla.

5 Heat a dry frying pan to a medium–high heat. One at a time, add the tortillas to the hot pan. Allow to cook for around 30–40 seconds, then flip the tortilla and immediately press down gently 3 or 4 times using a spatula. Cook for a further 20–30 seconds, then flip the tortilla back and press down gently again. Cook for a further 20–30 seconds.

6 Remove the cooked tortilla from the pan and set aside on a plate. Cover the plate loosely with a sheet of foil. As you cook each tortilla, add it to the stack and cover the plate with foil again. You can serve the wraps immediately, or allow them to cool completely and store for future use. They will keep well in the fridge for 1–2 days, or in the freezer for up to 1 month.

7 To reheat, wrap the tortillas in foil and bake in a preheated oven at 200°C/400°F/Gas Mark 6 for 10 minutes. Serve with any Mexican dish or use cold with any good sandwich filling.

Hummus

This dip makes an excellent starter served with toasted pitta breads and salad.

SERVES 2–3

1 x 400g tin of chickpeas, drained and rinsed
4 tablespoons Tahini Paste (see p.267)
2 garlic cloves
2 tablespoons lemon juice
Pinch of cayenne pepper
1 teaspoon cumin seeds
Sea salt and freshly ground black pepper

1   Put the chickpeas in a blender and pulse for 20–30 seconds until slightly blended. Add all the remaining ingredients, and season with sea salt and black pepper.
2   Blitz until the hummus reaches the desired consistency. If it is too thick, add a splash of water and blend again. Serve at room temperature with breadsticks or Pitta Salad (see p.94).

Tahini Paste (Kebab-shop style)

This paste is an essential ingredient in hummus or it can be
served with kebabs.

SERVES 2
300g/10½oz sesame seeds
180ml/6fl oz olive oil, plus extra to loosen if necessary

1 Toast the sesame seeds in a dry frying pan, or on a baking sheet in a
   hot oven (180°C/350°F/Gas Mark 4) for 5–6 minutes until just
   golden. Stir the seeds occasionally to ensure they toast evenly.
2 Put the toasted seeds in a blender with the olive oil. Blitz for 2
   minutes or until the paste reaches the desired consistency. Scrape
   the sides of the blender occasionally during blitzing to ensure all of
   the paste is mixed. Add more oil if required. The tahini paste will
   keep well in the fridge for 1–2 months.

Guacamole (Mexican-style)

This basic guacamole also works well with added chopped fresh tomatoes, garlic and chilli peppers. Place the avocado stones in the guacamole to keep the dip's bright green colour. For a thicker, more traditional guacamole, you can leave out the olive oil.

SERVES 1–2
2 ripe avocados, halved and destoned
½ small onion, finely chopped
1–2 tablespoons olive oil
¼ teaspoon sea salt
1 tablespoon lime juice

1 Scoop out the flesh from the avocado halves with a spoon and put it in a large bowl with the chopped onion, olive oil, sea salt and lime juice.
2 Mix the ingredients gently with a fork, mashing the avocado a little each time you stir. Serve with any Mexican dish or simply with tortilla chips.

Pico De Gallo

You can add cucumber, garlic, or even hot chilli sauce to this salsa if you like.

SERVES 1–2
2 large tomatoes, deseeded and chopped
1 small onion, chopped
1 finger chilli pepper, sliced
1 large handful coriander, chopped
¼ teaspoon sea salt
Pinch of black pepper
1–2 tablespoons lime juice

1   Quarter the tomatoes and use a spoon to remove the seeds. Roughly chop and place the bowl.
2   Combine all the ingredients in a large bowl until well mixed, then set aside for 1 hour to allow the flavours to mingle. Serve with any Mexican dish, or simply with tortilla chips.

Quesadilla (Mexican-style)

Any good Cheddar or mozzarella cheese will work very well in this recipe. Add serrano ham or sliced chilli peppers to the quesadilla, too, if you like.

SERVES 1–2
2 large flour tortillas
1 large handful of grated cheese

1   Heat a lightly oiled frying pan over a medium heat. Put one flour tortilla in the pan and cook for 30 seconds.
2   Turn the flour tortilla over and add the grated cheese evenly over the surface. Add the remaining flour tortilla and press down gently. Continue cooking for a further 1–2 minutes.
3   Flip the quesadilla over and cook for a further 1 minute. Remove the quesadilla from the pan and use a pizza cutter to slice into 4 large triangles. Serve with Pico De Gallo (see p.269).

Pastry Steak (Deli-style)

This hugely popular bakery snack is an excellent use of leftover stews and casseroles. The prepared stew may be frozen in portions for up to 3 months.

MAKES ENOUGH FOR 4 PASTRY STEAKS

2 teaspoons vegetable oil
2 large carrots, chopped
½ baby turnip (about 200g/7oz), chopped
1 large onion, chopped
500g/1lb 2 oz braising steak, diced
2 tablespoons plain flour
1 tablespoon tomato purée
2 teaspoons Worcestershire sauce
450ml/16fl oz beef stock, or 450ml/16fl oz boiling water mixed with
    1 beef stock cube
1 teaspoon dried mixed herbs
1 teaspoon dried parsley
400g/14oz puff pastry (uncooked weight)
1 egg, beaten
Sea salt and freshly ground black pepper

1   Heat half the vegetable oil in a large pan over a low–medium heat.
    Add the carrots, turnip and onion. Stir-fry for 5–6 minutes.
    Set aside.

2   In a large bowl, coat the braising steak in the flour and season with
    a pinch of sea salt. Heat the remaining oil in a frying pan over a high
    heat and brown the diced steak for 1–2 minutes, then tip the beef
    into the pan with the vegetables. Add the tomato purée and
    Worcestershire sauce and cook for a further 3–4 minutes. Add the
    beef stock, mixed herbs and parsley, along with a pinch of black
    pepper. Bring to the boil, reduce the heat to low and cover with a
    tight-fitting lid.

3 Simmer the beef stew for 1½–2 hours, adding a little water during cooking if it starts to look dry.

4 When the stew has cooked, remove the vegetables and eat or discard. Remove the beef pieces from the pan, allow to cool, then shred into tiny pieces and mix with the remaining gravy. You can now store the beef and gravy mixture in 3–4-tablespoon portions for use in future pastry steaks.

5 When you're ready to make the pastry steaks, preheat the oven to 220°C/425°F/ Gas Mark 7.

6 Divide the pastry into 4 equal pieces of 100g/3½oz each. Roll out each piece to a large square of roughly 15 x 15cm (6 x 6 inches). Add 3–4 tablespoons of beef-and-gravy mixture to one half of the pastry. Fold the remaining pastry over the mixture. Press the dough down firmly to seal, then crimp the edges with a fork. Repeat with the remaining portions of pastry and filling.

7 Place the pastry steaks on a baking tray and brush with beaten egg. Pierce the pastry steak in the centre with a knife in order to allow steam to escape during cooking. Bake the pastry steaks for 25 minutes or until the pastry is golden and cooked through and the filling is piping hot. Remove from the oven and leave to stand for 3–4 minutes before serving.

Prawn Cocktail (Bistro-style)

SERVES 1

1 little gem lettuce, leaves separated
100g/3½oz cooked, peeled prawns
2 tablespoons mayonnaise
4 teaspoons tomato ketchup
1 teaspoon Worcestershire sauce
1 teaspoon horseradish
Dash of Tabasco sauce
1 tablespoon lemon juice
Pinch of paprika powder, to serve
Sea salt and freshly ground black pepper

1 Line the inside of a glass with the lettuce leaves. Season the prawns with a little sea salt and pepper and spoon them into the glass on top of the lettuce.
2 Make a dressing. Combine the mayonnaise, ketchup, Worcestershire sauce, horseradish, Tabasco and lemon juice in a bowl, then season with sea salt and pepper to taste. Spoon the dressing into the glass on top of the prawns. Sprinkle with a little paprika and serve.

Prawn Cocktail (Bistro-style)

PART 7

Sweet Treats

What better way to round off the meal than with a delicious and indulgent dessert? Takeaway menus offer various treats, such as cookies, cakes and ice cream, that are irresistible but often highly priced. Of course, preparing your own desserts keeps the cost down (but I can't promise that it will do anything to encourage you to resist temptation).

Many people feel more apprehensive about cooking desserts than they do savoury foods, believing that you need experience and the patience to weigh out everything precisely, mix the ingredients in a particular order and then bake them for not a minute longer than the recipe states. But I think that even a novice cook can create delicious cakes and biscuits with just a little know-how. Following a few simple tips will make sure that everything goes to plan.

When recipes for cakes or biscuits call for butter or margarine, use a vegetable-based baking margarine, which will be less expensive than premium butters, is the spread of choice in many bakeries, and will deliver excellent results.

While you can use expensive or high-cocoa-content chocolate if you like, inexpensive brands will also offer very good results, so feel free to make your ingredient choice based on budget and availability.

You can prepare most of the desserts included in this chapter in advance, and many of them will freeze beautifully, making life easier when you're looking for that takeaway fast-food fix. It also means you can ration out the chocolate fudge cake so that you can eat it over the course of a few weeks as opposed to a few days – in theory, at least, if you have the willpower to resist!

Apple Pie Slices (American Fast-food Style)

If serving immediately, warn your guests that the filling will be very hot!

SERVES 2

3 apples, peeled and cut into small dice
1½ tablespoons white sugar
1 tablespoon brown sugar
Pinch of cinnamon
Dash of lemon juice
2 tablespoons water
½ teaspoon cornflour mixed with 1 tablespoon water
120g/4oz plain flour, plus extra for dusting
Small pinch of salt
60g/4oz salted butter, cubed and chilled
Vegetable oil, for deep frying
2 teaspoons caster sugar, to serve

1   Place the apple pieces in a small pan and add both lots of sugar, the cinnamon, lemon juice and water. Mix well. Cook the apples over a low heat for 8–10 minutes or until soft, stirring often. When the apples have softened, add the cornflour and water mixture, mix well once again and simmer for a further 2 minutes. Mash the apple mixture well and set aside to cool.
2   Put the plain flour and salt in a large bowl. Mix well. Add the butter and work into the flour until well combined. Add the water and stir until you have a pastry dough. Tip out the pastry on to a flour-dusted work surface and use a rolling pin to roll it into a thin, rough rectangular shape.
3   Cut 2 pastry squares strips from the dough, each about 15 x 15cm (6 x 6 inches) in size. Heap the apple mixture into one half of both pastry squares, leaving a margin along the edge of the filled side.

Use a little water to moisten the other half of each pastry square and fold the empty half over on top of the filling. Press down along the edges of the dough to seal the filling, then use a fork to create a crimped effect.

4   When you're ready to cook the pie slices, set your deep fryer to 180°C/350°F. Alternatively, fill a wok or large frying pan one third full with vegetable oil and heat to 180°C/350°F. The oil is ready when a few breadcrumbs dropped into the oil sizzle immediately. Drop in the apple pie slices and fry for 3–4 minutes, turning occasionally, until golden all over. Remove from the pan and drain off any excess oil.

5   Sprinkle the apple pie slices with caster sugar and serve immediately or cool to room temperature and eat cold.

Banana Muffins (British-bakery Style)

These muffins freeze extremely well, making them ideal to defrost each night and take to work the following day.

MAKES 12–14
180g/6oz plain flour
1 teaspoon baking powder
1 teaspoon bicarbonate of soda (baking soda)
½ teaspoon salt
3 ripe bananas, mashed
150g/5oz white sugar
1 egg
1 teaspoon vanilla extract
75ml/2½fl oz vegetable oil

1 Preheat the oven to 190°C/375°F/Gas Mark 5.
2 Put the plain flour, baking powder, bicarbonate of soda and salt in a large bowl and mix well to combine.
3 Put the mashed banana in a separate bowl, add the the remaining ingredients and mix well.
4 Add the wet ingredients to the dry ingredients and mix thoroughly until well combined.
5 Lightly oil two muffin trays. Pour a large tablespoon of the mixture into each muffin space and bake for 18–20 minutes. Check that the muffins are completely cooked by piercing the centre of a muffin with a fork. The muffins are ready when the fork comes out clean.
6 Remove the muffins from the oven and leave to rest for 5 minutes before removing from the trays and arranging on a wire rack to cool completely. The muffins will freeze well for up to 1 month.

Chocolate Orange Muffins (British-bakery Style)

Quick, easy and delicious.

MAKES 8

300g/10½oz chocolate and hazelnut spread
2 large eggs
100g/3½oz self-raising flour
3–4 tablespoons whole milk
1 teaspoon natural orange flavouring
3–4 tablespoons chocolate chips (optional)
Buttercream or icing, as desired

1 Preheat the oven to 180°C/350°F/Gas Mark 4.
2 In a large mixing bowl, combine the chocolate and hazelnut spread, eggs, self-raising flour, milk and orange flavouring. Mix well until smooth. Add the chocolate chips (if using) and mix once more until the chips are suspended evenly throughout the mixture.
3 Line an 8-hole cupcake tray with paper cases and spoon equal amounts of the mixture into each case. Bake the muffins for about 20–25 minutes or until a fork inserted into a muffin comes out clean. Allow to cool in the tray for 2–3 minutes, then remove to a wire rack to cool completely.
4 Top with buttercream or icing, or simply serve plain with cream or ice cream.

Sticky Toffee Pudding
(British-bakery Style)

MAKES 1 LARGE PUDDING
150g/5oz pitted dried dates
250ml/9fl oz weak black tea
½ teaspoon bicarbonate of soda (baking soda)
200g/7oz golden caster sugar
2 eggs, whisked
100g/3½oz vegetable oil margarine
200g/7oz self-raising flour
1 teaspoon mixed spice
1 teaspoon vanilla extract
200ml/7fl oz double cream
1 x 397g/14oz tin of dulce de leche (milk-based caramel sauce)

1   Preheat the oven to 180°C/350°F/Gas Mark 4.
2   Chop the dates and place them in a large pan over a medium heat.
    Add the tea and simmer for 2–3 minutes or until the dates have
    softened. Reduce the heat to low and add the bicarbonate of soda.
    The mixture will become fizzy – don't panic! This is what we want
    to happen! Switch off the heat, stir once and set aside.
3   In a large bowl, combine the sugar, eggs and vegetable oil
    margarine. Mix well. Add half the self-raising flour and mix until
    fully incorporated into the mixture, then add the remaining flour,
    along with the mixed spice and vanilla extract. Mix thoroughly
    again.
4   Add the dates to the mix. If you prefer a smoother texture, press the
    date mixture through a sieve before doing so. Pour the mixture into
    a greased 25 x 25cm (10 x 10-inch) square cake tin and bake in the
    oven for 35–40 minutes or until a skewer inserted into the centre
    comes out clean.
5   Remove the cake tin from the oven and set aside to cool for 5
    minutes. Remove the pudding from the cake tin and set on a wire

rack. You can serve the pudding straightaway, or allow it to cool completely, then reheat briefly in the microwave or oven before serving.

6   Pour the double cream and dulce de leche into a saucepan and warm gently over a low heat, stirring frequently until a smooth sauce is created. The prepared sauce will keep well in the fridge for several days if desired. Place a portion of the sticky toffee pudding in a large bowl and pour over the prepared sauce. Serve with ice cream or custard.

Chocolate Chip Cookies (Bakery-style)

These are chewy cookies, packed with chocolate chips. Serve with coffee for brunch or with ice cold milk for a late supper. Replace 50g/2oz of the self-raising flour with 50g/2oz of cocoa powder if you like, for a double chocolate version. The cookie dough freezes well – and you can use it immediately if you slice the dough into cookies before you freeze. If cooking from frozen allow an extra 3–4 minutes cooking time.

MAKES 10–12
125g/4oz butter
100g/3½oz caster sugar
100g/3½oz light brown sugar
1 egg
1 teaspoon vanilla extract
225g/8oz self-raising flour
½ teaspoon salt
100g/3½oz chocolate chips

1 In a large bowl, combine the butter, caster sugar and brown sugar. Mix thoroughly until the butter and sugar are well combined, then add the egg and vanilla extract and mix thoroughly once more.
2 Add the flour, salt and chocolate chips. Mix well so that the chips are distributed evenly throughout the mixture, and shape into a long log shape, then refrigerate the dough for 2 hours.
3 Preheat the oven to 180°C/350°F/Gas Mark 4. Remove the cookie dough from the fridge and slice into individual cookies. Place the slices on a baking tray and bake for 7–8 minutes (or 3–4 minutes longer if cooking from frozen), until just cooked through. Remove

the finished cookies from the oven and leave to rest for 2–3 minutes. The cookies will be very soft at first, but should become slightly more firm as they cool down. Serve immediately or place on a wire rack to cool completely.

Warm Cookie Dough (American Fast-food Style)

Crispy on the outside, soft and chewy in the middle, this warm dessert has become a hugely popular addition to pizza restaurant menus.

MAKES 4 PORTIONS
125g/4oz butter
100g/3½ oz caster sugar
100g/3½oz brown sugar
1 egg
1 teaspoon vanilla extract
175g/6oz self-raising flour
½ teaspoon salt
50g/2oz cocoa powder
100g/3½oz white chocolate chips

1   Combine the butter, caster sugar and brown sugar in a large bowl, then add the egg and vanilla extract and stir. Add the flour, salt, cocoa powder and white chocolate chips. Mix well until the dough comes together.
2   Preheat the oven to 200°C/400°F/Gas Mark 6. Divide the cookie mixture into 4 portions. Press out one portion of cookie dough into a 18cm (7-inch) diameter round cake tin (a round takeaway foil tray is a good option – they are readily available in packs of 5 at super-markets). Repeat the process with the remaining cookie dough, or refrigerate or freeze for future use.
3   Bake the cookie dough into the oven for 6 minutes, then reduce the oven temperature to 180°C/350°F/Gas Mark 4 and continue to bake for a further 6–8 minutes or until the dough is golden on the top and just cooked through inside. Remove the warm cookie dough from the oven and allow to cool for 3–4 minutes before serving with vanilla ice cream.

Empire Biscuits (British-bakery Style)

Also known as 'double biscuits', these are a bakery classic.

MAKES 12–15
200g/7fl oz vegetable oil margarine
125g/4½oz caster sugar
1 egg yolk
2 teaspoons vanilla extract, plus extra for the icing (optional)
275g/10oz plain flour, plus extra for dusting
2 tablespoons raspberry jam
2 tablespoons raspberry dessert sauce
240g/8½oz icing sugar
15 jelly tot sweets or glacé cherries

1 Preheat the oven to 180°C/350°F/Gas Mark 4.
2 In a large bowl, combine the vegetable oil margarine, sugar,
   egg yolk and vanilla extract. Mix well. Slowly add the flour and mix
   well until you form a dough – you may not need all the flour.
3 Use your hands to press the mixture together and knead until the
   dough becomes smooth. If the mixture is too crumbly, add a little
   more vegetable oil margarine and knead again. Once the dough
   comes together, stop kneading so that the heat from your hands
   does not melt the spread.
4 Roll out the dough on a floured work surface to a thickness of
   around 5–7.5mm (¼ inch). Cut circles out of the dough using a
   pastry cutter or the rim of a mug and place the rounds on a lightly
   greased baking tray.
5 Place the tray in the preheated oven and bake for about 10 minutes
   or until the biscuits are golden brown. The biscuits may seem soft
   when removed from the oven but will harden as they cool. Once
   they have cooled for a few minutes on the baking tray, use a spatula
   to lift them on to a wire rack and set aside to cool completely.

6   In a small bowl, combine the raspberry jam and raspberry
    dessert sauce. Add 1–2 teaspoons of the mixture to half of the
    cooled biscuits and place the remaining biscuit halves on top to
    form a biscuit sandwich.
7   Sieve the icing sugar into a bowl and whisk in 220ml/7¾fl oz of
    water until smooth and pourable, then stir in a dash of vanilla
    extract, if you wish. Spread 1 tablespoon of the icing over the top of
    each biscuit. Top with a jelly tot sweet or glacé cherry and serve.
    The biscuits will keep well for 2 days in a sealed container.

Chocolate Fudge Cake (American-diner Style)

MAKES 1 LARGE CAKE
300g/10½oz plain flour
50g/2oz cocoa powder
1 teaspoon bicarbonate of soda (baking soda)
1 teaspoon salt
125g/4½oz butter
300g/10½oz caster sugar
2 eggs
1 teaspoon vanilla extract
3 teaspoons white vinegar
About 200ml/7fl oz semi-skimmed milk

FOR THE CHOCOLATE BUTTER ICING:
75g/2½oz unsalted butter
175g/6oz icing sugar
3–4 tablespoons cocoa powder
Semi-skimmed milk

1   Preheat the oven to 180°C/350°F/Gas Mark 4.
2   Sieve the plain flour, cocoa powder, bicarbonate of soda and salt into a large bowl and mix thoroughly.
3   In a separate large bowl, cream the butter and caster sugar until fluffy. Add the eggs and vanilla extract and mix thoroughly.
4   Add the wet ingredients to the dry ingredients and beat to a smooth cake batter. Add the vinegar and beat again, then add the milk and beat again ensuring no lumps remain.
5   Divide the mixture between two 20cm (8-inch) diameter round, non-stick cake tins. Bake for about 20 minutes or until a skewer inserted into the middle comes out clean.
6   Remove the cake tins from the oven and set the cakes aside to cool in the tins for 8–10 minutes, before transferring the cakes to a wire rack to cool completely.

7 Make the chocolate butter icing by combining the unsalted butter, icing sugar and cocoa powder in a large bowl. Mix thoroughly, slowly adding semi-skimmed milk a tablespoon at a time until you have a medium–thick consistency. Spread the chocolate butter cream over one half of the cake. Add the top half of the cake and spread with the remaining butter icing.

8 Cut the cake into slices and serve. Individual slices will freeze well in small foil containers for up to 1 month. If you like, you can heat the cake slices in a microwave for 15 seconds until just warm, then serve with vanilla ice cream.

Chocolate Brownies (American-diner Style)

These brownies are made using dark chocolate chips, but you can use white or milk chocolate, if you prefer.

MAKES 12 BROWNIES

400g/14oz dark chocolate (minimum 60% cocoa solids), broken into pieces
250g/8oz vegetable oil margarine
350g/12oz caster sugar
4 large eggs, lightly beaten
1 teaspoon vanilla extract
200g/7oz plain flour
1½ teaspoons baking powder

1   Line a large cake tin with baking paper. Preheat the oven to 190°C/375°F/Gas Mark 5.

2   Put 250g/8oz of the chocolate in a pan on a very low heat. Stir the chocolate frequently and remove from the heat just before fully melted so that the residual heat finishes the melting process. Set aside to cool slightly (you don't want it to scramble the eggs when you add it to the cake batter).

3   In a large bowl, cream together the vegetable oil margarine and sugar until light and fluffy. Add the eggs and vanilla extract, stir, then add the melted chocolate, ensuring that it has sufficiently cooled so that it doesn't scramble the eggs. Add the plain flour and baking powder and mix to fully combine. Finally, gently stir through the remaining chocolate pieces, a few at a time.

4   Pour the brownie mixture into a lined cake tin. Place the tin in the preheated oven on the middle shelf and bake for 40–50 minutes. To check the brownies, gently shake the cake tin from side to side. If the mixture is wobbly, return it to the oven for another few minutes. Remove the cake tin from the oven and allow to cool for 5 minutes.

5   Remove the brownie from the cake tin and peel off any baking paper while still warm in order to prevent it from sticking. Place the brownie on a wire rack and allow it to cool completely. Cut the brownie into 12 large squares and serve.

Easy Chocolate Cheesecake (American-diner Style)

This instant chocolate cheesecake uses only 4 ingredients and you can have it ready in just a few minutes.

SERVES 1

4 digestive biscuits
2 tablespoons butter
3 tablespoons chocolate and hazelnut spread, plus extra to taste
2 tablespoons soft cheese, plus extra to taste

1   Put the digestive biscuits in a blender and blitz into crumbs, then transfer the crumbs to a mixing bowl.
2   Melt the butter in a small pan over a low heat, then slowly combine it with the biscuit crumbs. Press the mixture into an 8 x 5cm (3¼ x 2-inch) dessert ring and pat down firmly.
3   In a bowl, combine the chocolate and hazelnut spread and soft cheese. Mix well. Taste and add more chocolate or cheese, if you like. Spoon the chocolate and cheese mixture onto the top of the biscuit base. Refrigerate for 2–3 hours or until set. Remove the dessert ring carefully, then slice and serve.

Ambassador's Chocolates (American-diner Style)

With these crispy, nutty chocolates you'll really spoil yourself and your guests!

MAKES 4–6 CHOCOLATES
3 plain crispbreads
2 tablespoons chocolate and hazelnut spread

1 Crush the crispbreads in a blender or with a rolling pin.
2 Gently warm the chocolate and hazelnut spread in the microwave for a few seconds.
3 Pour the blended crispbreads into a mug and add the chocolate and hazelnut spread. Mix thoroughly.
4 Spoon the mixture into 4–6 petits fours cases and refrigerate for 2 hours or until set before serving.

Churros with Chocolate Cream Sauce (American-diner Style)

Also known as 'Spanish Doughnuts' (although often sold in Mexican restaurants), these sweet fried pastries are best eaten warm.

SERVES 2–3

1 tablespoon vegetable oil, plus extra for deep frying

Pinch of salt

1 teaspoon caster sugar

120g/4oz plain flour

Pinch of baking powder

2 tablespoons caster sugar mixed with a pinch of ground cinnamon

2 tablespoons chocolate and hazelnut spread

1 tablespoon double cream

4 tablespoons semi-skimmed milk

1   In a small pan, combine the vegetable oil, salt and caster sugar with 200ml/7fl oz of water, then bring to the boil over a medium heat. Once boiling, remove from the heat.

2   Combine the flour and baking powder and mix well. Slowly add the flour mixture to the liquid, whisking thoroughly until you have created a smooth thick batter. Set aside for 10 minutes.

3   Put the batter into a piping bag and attach a star-shaped nozzle.

4   When you're ready to cook the churros, set your deep fryer to 180°C/350°F. Alternatively, fill a wok or large frying pan one third full with vegetable oil and heat to 180°C/350°F. The oil is ready when a few breadcrumbs dropped into the oil sizzle immediately. Once hot, carefully pipe several long strips of batter into the hot oil. Fry the churros for around 2–3 minutes per side or until cooked through and golden. (If you don't have a piping bag, take a small handful of the batter mixture and roll it between your hands into a

long thin sausage shape. Repeat until you have used all the batter and fry as above.

5   Remove the cooked churros from the pan and drain off any excess oil on kitchen paper. Roll the churros in the caster sugar and cinnamon mixture.

6   In a small pan, combine the chocolate and hazelnut spread, double cream and semi-skimmed milk. Place over a low heat, stir and bring to a simmer for 3–4 minutes or until the sauce thickens slightly.

7   Arrange the churros on a plate and serve with the chocolate cream sauce on the side.

Deep-fried Mars Bar (Chip-shop Style)

Some may say that this dish could only have been invented in Scotland! Surprisingly light and delicious, it's a dessert that has to be tried at least once!

SERVES 1

120g/4oz plain flour
60g/2oz cornflour
Small pinch of bicarbonate of soda (baking soda)
About 200ml/7fl oz beer
Vegetable oil, for deep frying
1 Mars bar, refrigerated

1 In a large bowl, combine the plain flour, cornflour and bicarbonate of soda. Mix well. Slowly add the beer, whisking thoroughly until the batter becomes smooth and is the consistency of single cream (You may not need all the beer.)

2 When you're ready to cook the Mars bar, set your deep fryer to 180°C/350°F. Alternatively, fill a wok or large frying pan one third full with vegetable oil and heat to 180°C/350°F. The oil is ready when a few breadcrumbs dropped into the oil sizzle immediately.

3 Take the Mars bar out of the fridge, unwrap it and rinse it under cold water. Dip it into the batter until completely coated, then place it carefully into the hot oil. Deep-fry the Mars bar for 1–2 minutes or until golden on all sides. Remove from the pan and drain off any excess oil on kitchen paper.

4 Place the Mars bar on a plate and slice into 2 pieces. The batter should be light and crisp and the Mars bar just slightly melted on the inside. Serve on its own or with ice cream.

Salt 'n' Sweet Popcorn

There is nothing like the smell of freshly made popcorn. This recipe satisfies both those with a savoury and with a sweet tooth. Made in minutes and amounting to only pennies per portion, it's the perfect snack for your home cinema nights.

SERVES 2
4 tablespoons vegetable oil
8 tablespoons popping corn
2 tablespoons brown sugar
Salt, to taste

1 Heat the oil in a large pan with a lid (leave the lid off for now) until almost smoking.
2 Add the popping corn and stir immediately to coat the corn with oil. As soon as the corn looks as though it's about to start popping, add the brown sugar and put the lid on. Shake the pan continuously over the heat as the corn pops to ensure the sugar doesn't burn and is evenly distributed over the popcorn. Keep shaking until the popping slows down and all of the corn has popped.
3 Remove the pan from the heat and set aside for 1 minute. Pour the popcorn into a large container. Season to taste with salt and serve.

Vanilla Ice Cream (American-diner Style)

This homemade ice cream, made soft with semi-skimmed milk, will rival the finest restaurant-bought variety.

SERVES 2–3
120ml/4fl oz semi-skimmed milk
50g/2oz white sugar
2 teaspoons vanilla extract
120ml/4fl oz double cream

1   In a bowl, combine the semi-skimmed milk, white sugar and vanilla extract. Mix well.
2   In a separate bowl, whisk the cream until it forms soft peaks. Add the cream to the milk-and-sugar mixture and mix well once again.
3   Pour the mixture into an ice cream maker and churn according to the machine instructions.
4   Alternatively, make the ice cream by hand. Place the mixture into a freezer-proof tub and place in the freezer. After 40 minutes, stir the mixture well, breaking up any ice crystals that have formed. Mix until the mixture becomes smooth again. Place the tub back in the freezer and repeat the mixing process every 40–45 minutes until the ice cream is completely smooth and frozen.
5   Freeze as normal. Serve with hot chocolate sauce or simply with wafers.

Hot Chocolate (American-diner Style)

Serve up this easy hot chocolate with grated dark chocolate or marshmallows, or simply on its own to warm up a cold night.

SERVES 1
½ tablespoon cocoa powder
½ tablespoon sugar
1 tablespoon water
½ cinnamon stick
230ml/8fl oz semi-skimmed milk
Dash of vanilla extract
Grated dark chocolate and marshmallows, to serve (optional)

1 In a serving bowl or cup, combine the cocoa powder, sugar and water. Mix well to form a paste.
2 Put the cinnamon stick and semi-skimmed milk in a small pan. Heat over a medium heat until the milk just comes to the boil, then strain the milk through a sieve and pour into the cocoa powder, sugar and water mixture. Mix well until all of the ingredients are fully combined.
3 Add the vanilla extract, stir through, and top with a sprinkling of dark chocolate and marshmallows (if using), then serve.

Index

thin-crust pizza base 223
tikka masala sauce 195
toast, prawn 115
tomatoes: chilli con carne 57–8
  chilli non carne vegetable chilli
    59–60
  instant pizza sauce 226
  Italian pizza sauce 224
  kebab-shop pizza 92
  margherita pizza 227
  marinara sauce 10–11
  pico de gallo 269
  salsa 63–4
  spaghetti bolognese 235–6
  sweet pizza sauce 225
  see also ketchup
tortilla chips: loaded jalapeño
    nachos 63–4
tortillas: chicken fajita wrap
    258–9
  quesadilla 270
  tortilla wraps 265
tuna mayonnaise sandwich 260
turmeric rice 213
tzatziki 100

V
vanilla ice cream 298
vanilla shake 65
vegetables: baby vegetable pakora
    173–4
  mixed vegetable chop suey 153–4
  mixed vegetable curry 197
  mixed vegetable rice 214
  see also peppers, tomatoes etc
vegetarian stuffed-crust pizza 230
veggie volcano 231

W
warm cookie dough 285
whopping big burger 28–9
wontons, deep-fried 116
wraps: chicken fajita wrap 258–9
  tortilla wraps 265

Y
yakitori chicken 252–3
yogurt: lassi 216
  pakora sauce 178
  raita 179
  tzatziki 100